This book belongs to the collection of

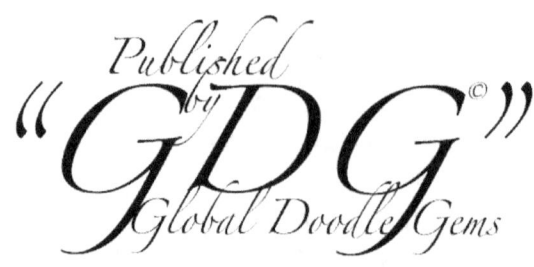

Share your colored versions with us ! We love seeing your results and hearing from you we are social !

The Official FB book page, stay on top of what we have in the works !
www.facebook.com/globaldoodlegems
The Community group, share your colored pages, meet the artists, enjoy exclusive freebies, take part in community Charity books and so much more......
www.facebook.com/groups/globaldoodlegems/
Follow us on Twitter.... @GlobalDoodlegem
We are on Instagram too
@globaldoodlegems for instagram
...and if you are not social like that we have a blog
globaldoodlegems.wordpress.com

Copyright © 2018 Global Doodle Gems
All rights are reserved by Global Doodle Gems.
Duplication of pages for personal use are allowed. You are invited to color the pages then scan/post your coloured versions to social networks, mentioning the book title and author/artist (Global Doodle Gems).
All artwork and images are protected by copyright laws. This book or any portion thereof may not, otherwise, be reproduced and/or distributed or transmitted without the express written permission of the artist/publisher of Global Doodle Gems.
All of us from the Global Doodle Gems wish you a colortastic time and look forward to seeing your wonderful color results online !

Welcome to my book Mandala 2

I hope you will enjoy the 50 Mandalas in my book.
I colored for the Cover on my Patreon site, here my Patreons get access to new work early and to live video's where I color for my coming books, I also do live drawing there, wo you can follow a drawing from the first lines on the paper to my final colored result ...and color along with me, this is a lot of fun times with great interaction.

You can find my Patreon here
https://www.patreon.com/amvwart

You can also find my artpage on Facebook here
https://www.facebook.com/AMVWART/

I have an ongoing Color A Weirdie A Day project, where we color live daily the weirdie of the day, you can find the group here
www.facebook.com/groups/ColorAWeirdieADay

I also have a Youtube Channel here you can find video previews of all my books and of books published with Global Doodle Gems, you can also find coloring and drawing video's here
https://www.youtube.com/c/amvwart

Most of my books are available as pdf versions as well, I am all the time adding more books to my Payhip shop, so be sure to check it out, there are usually great discounts available on the pdf's here
https://payhip.com/amvwart

Wishing all a wonderful and creative time with lot's
of beautiful colors and smiles

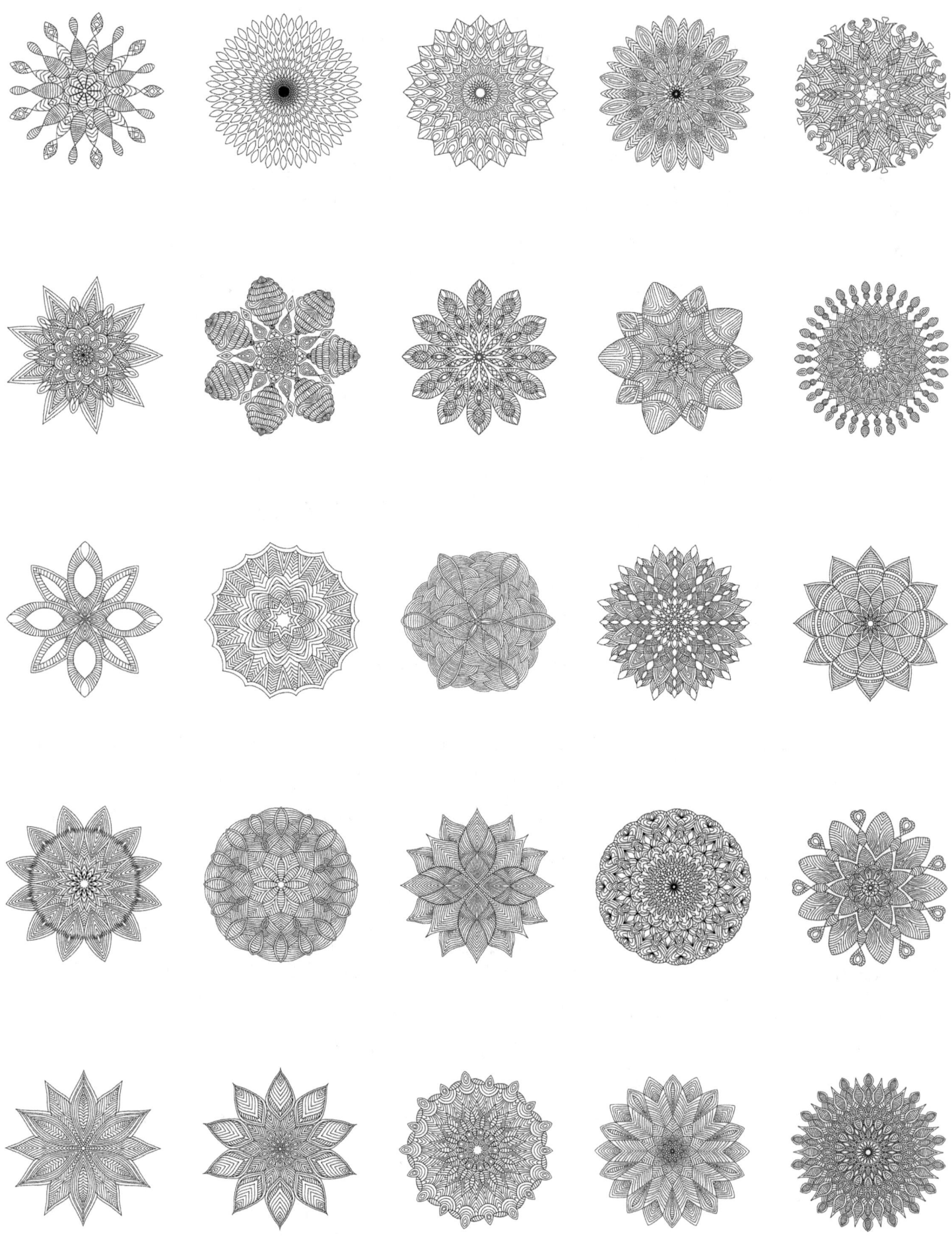

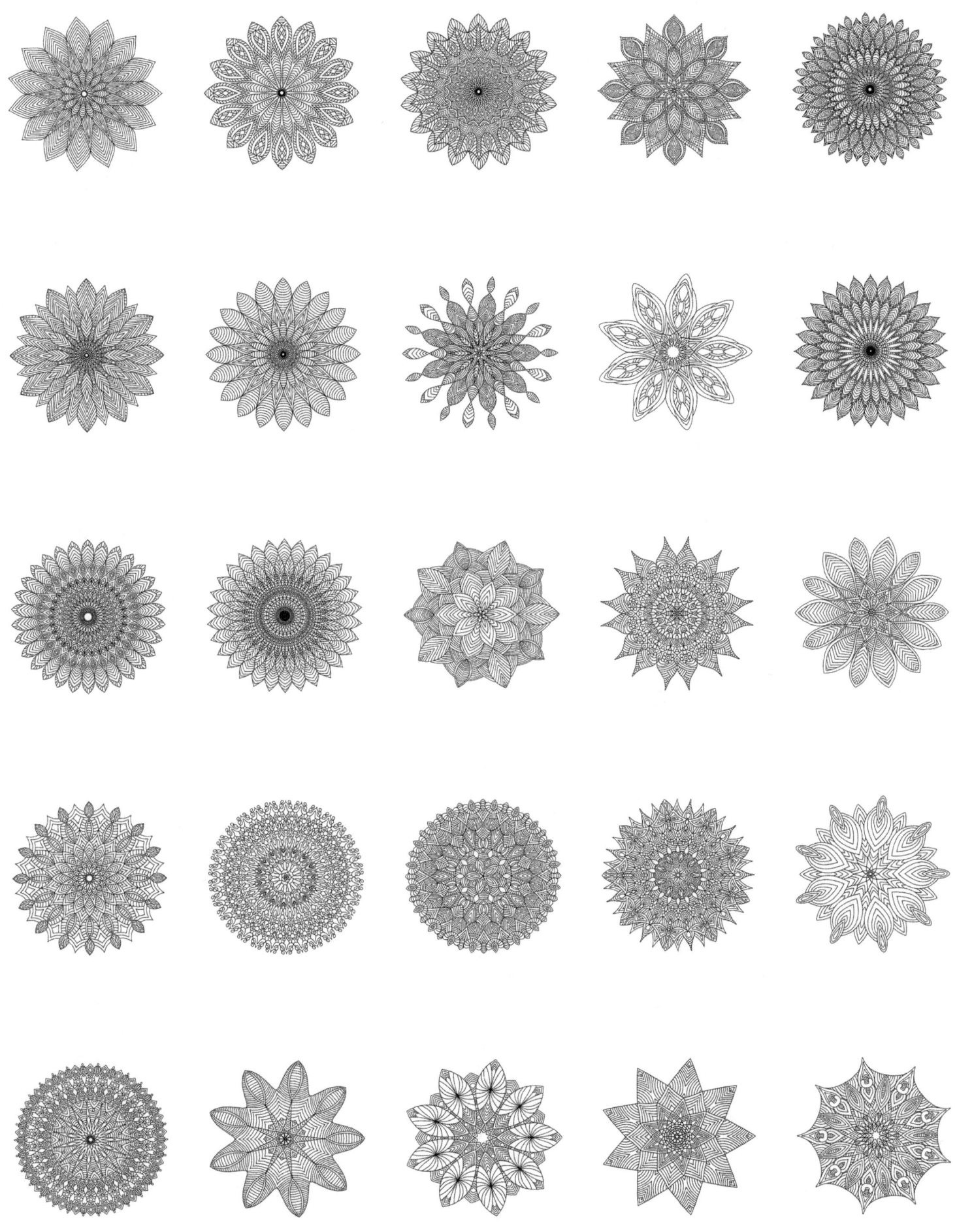

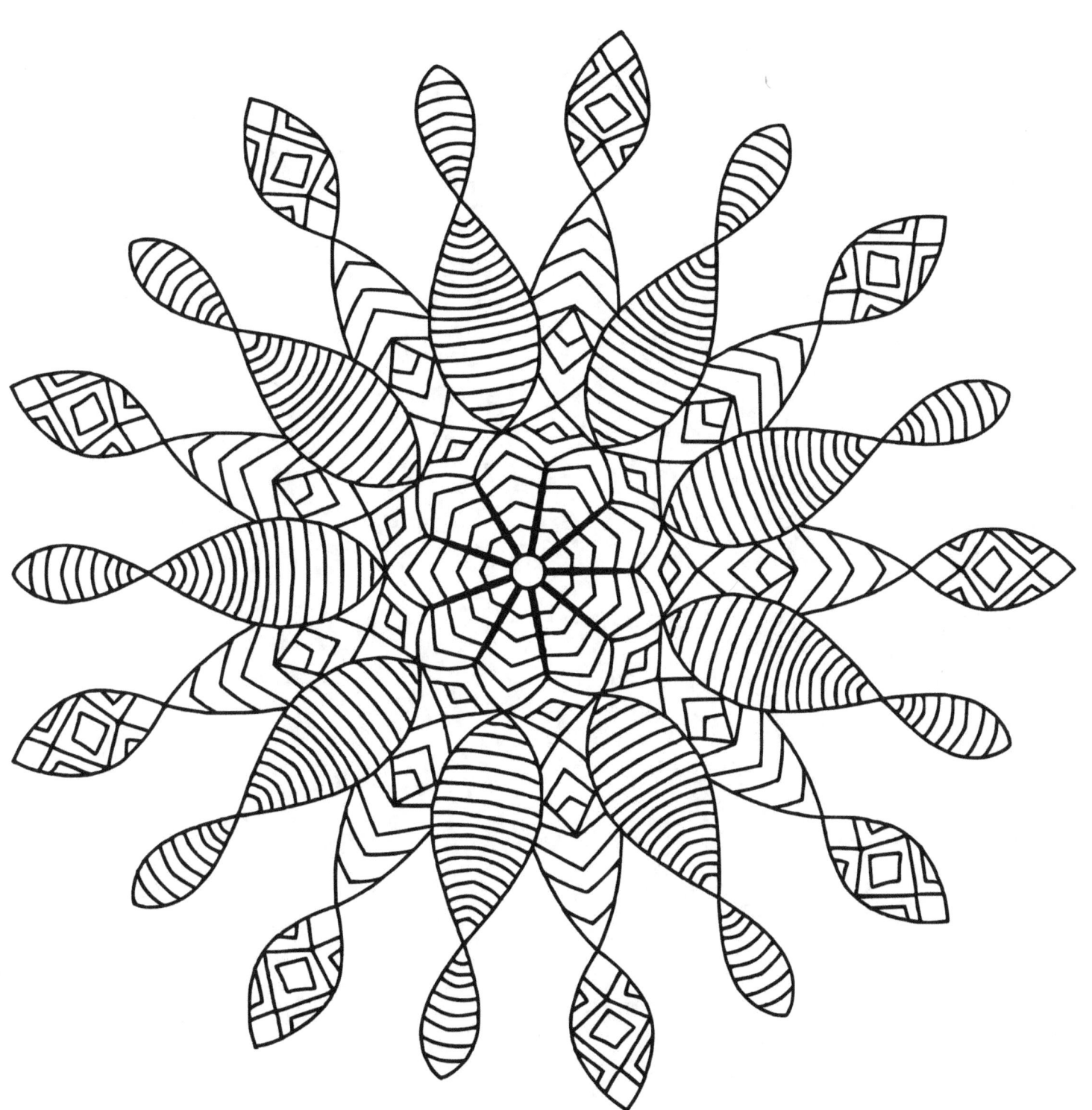

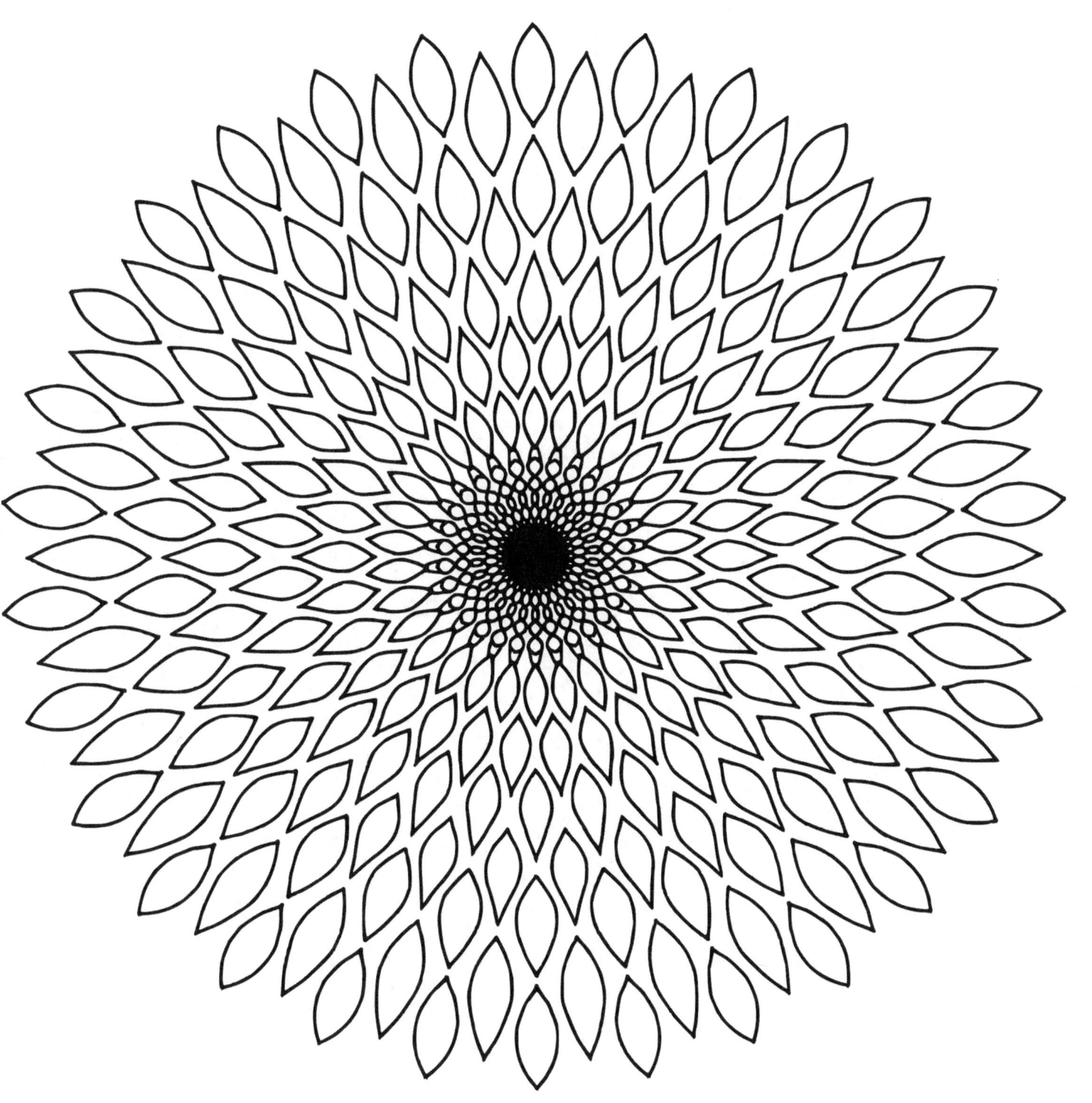

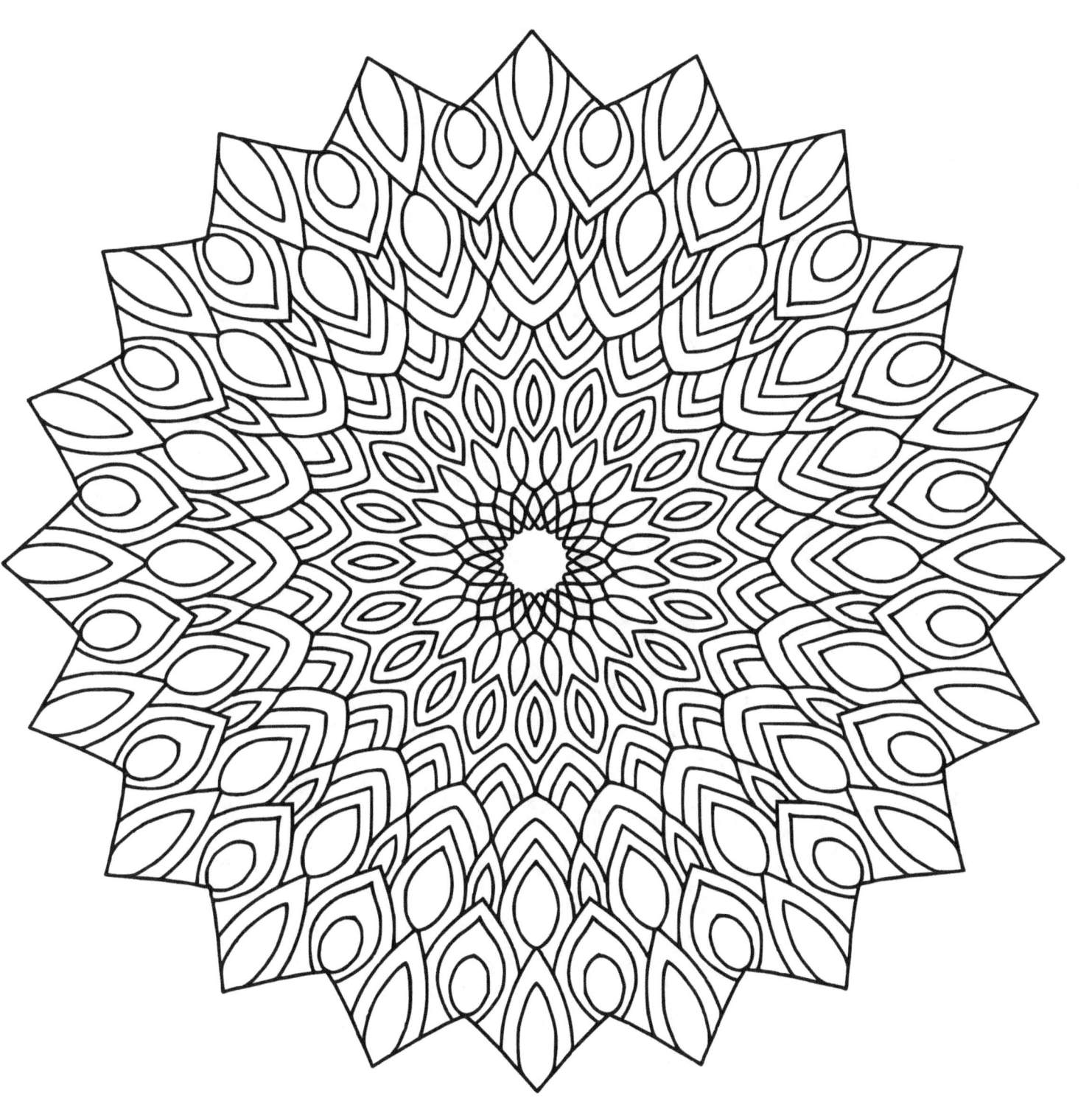

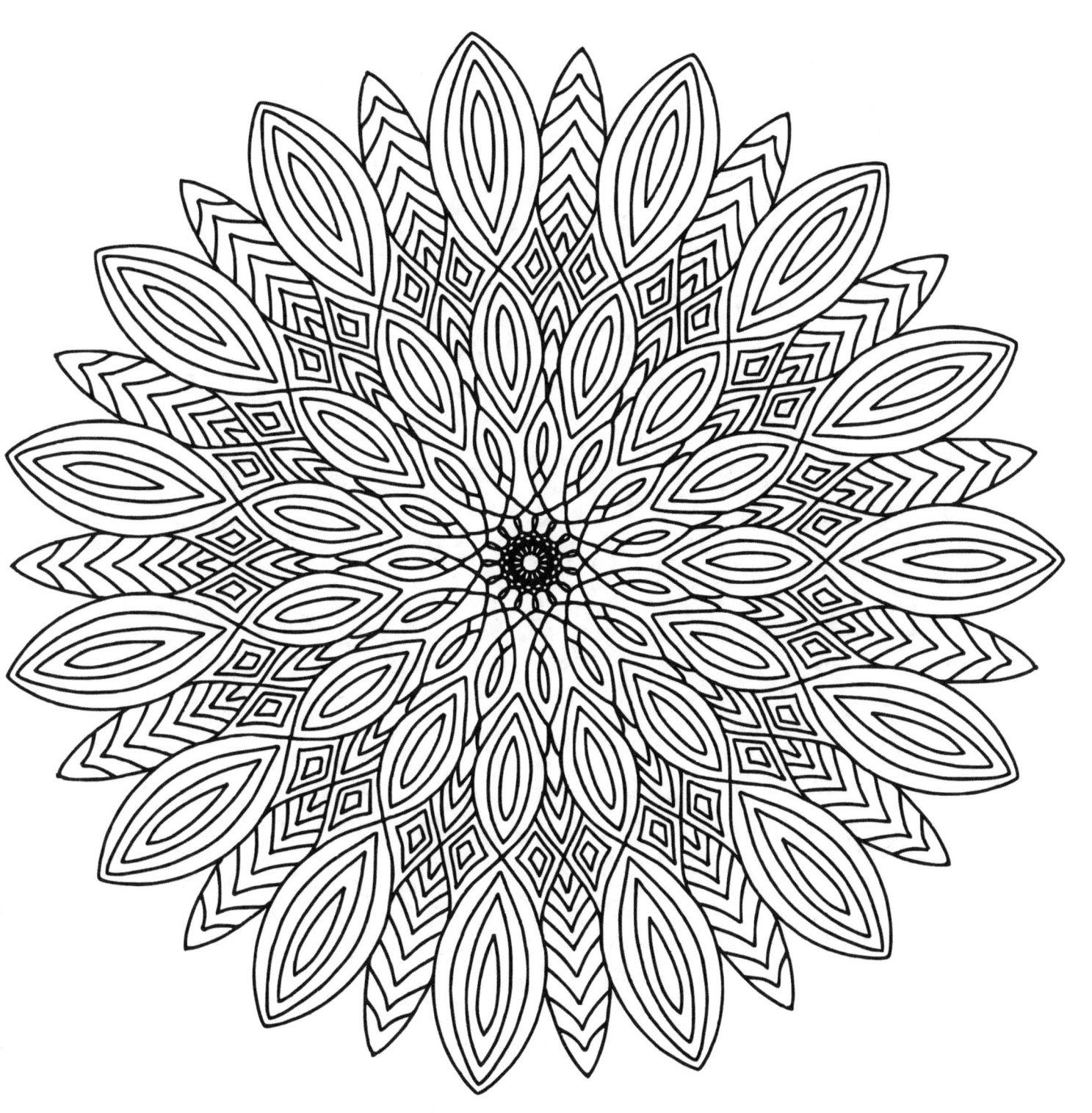

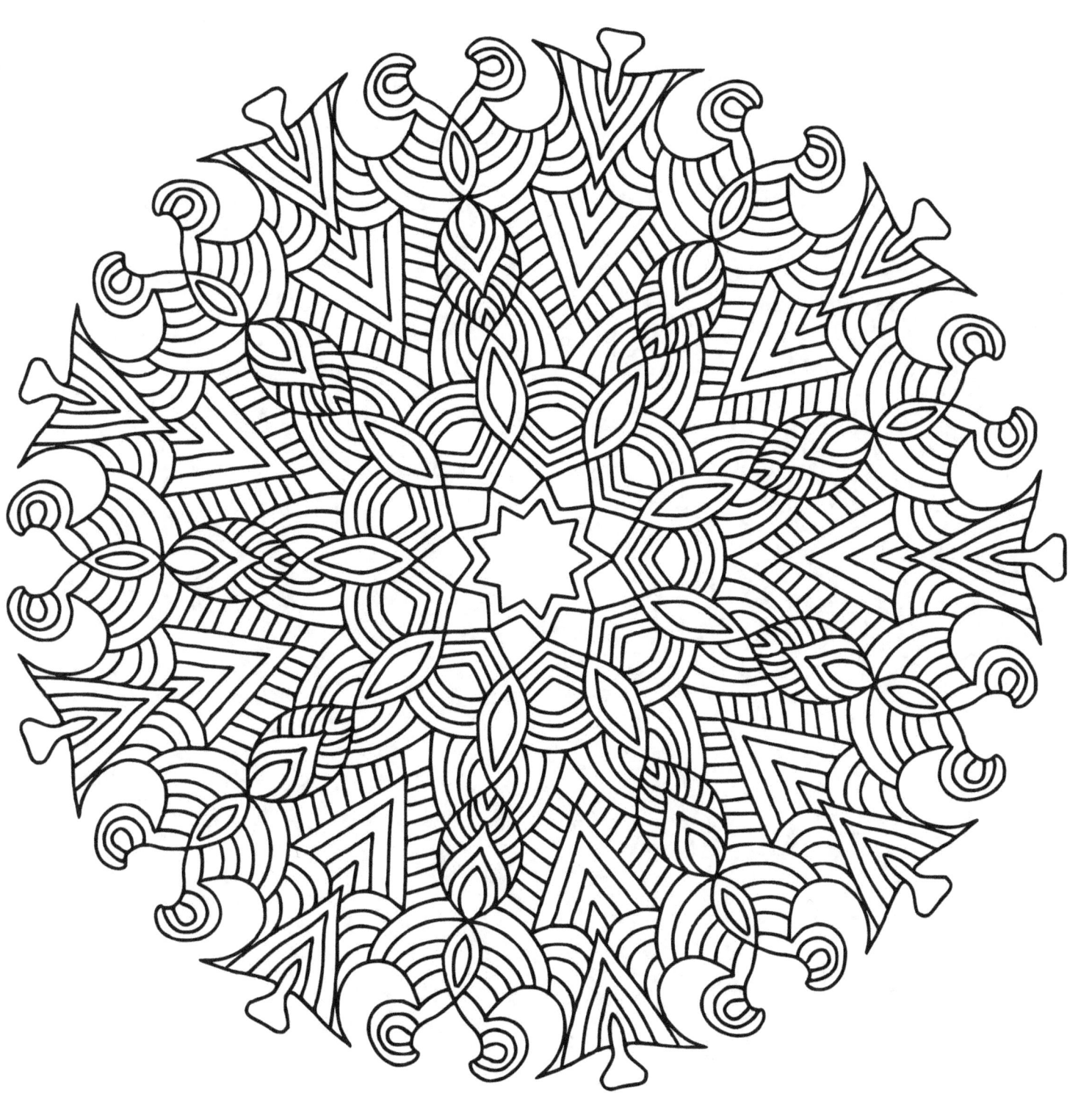

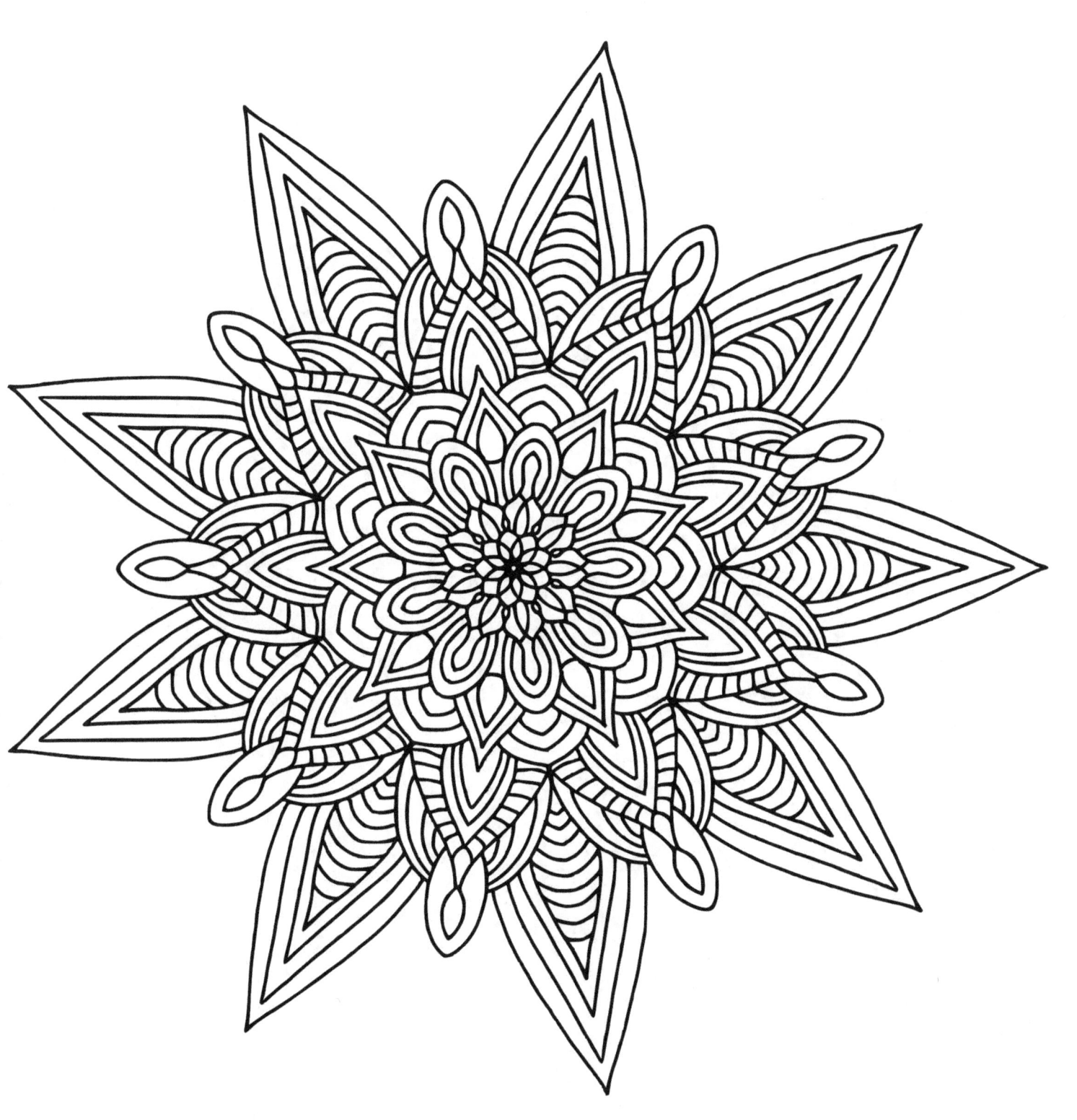

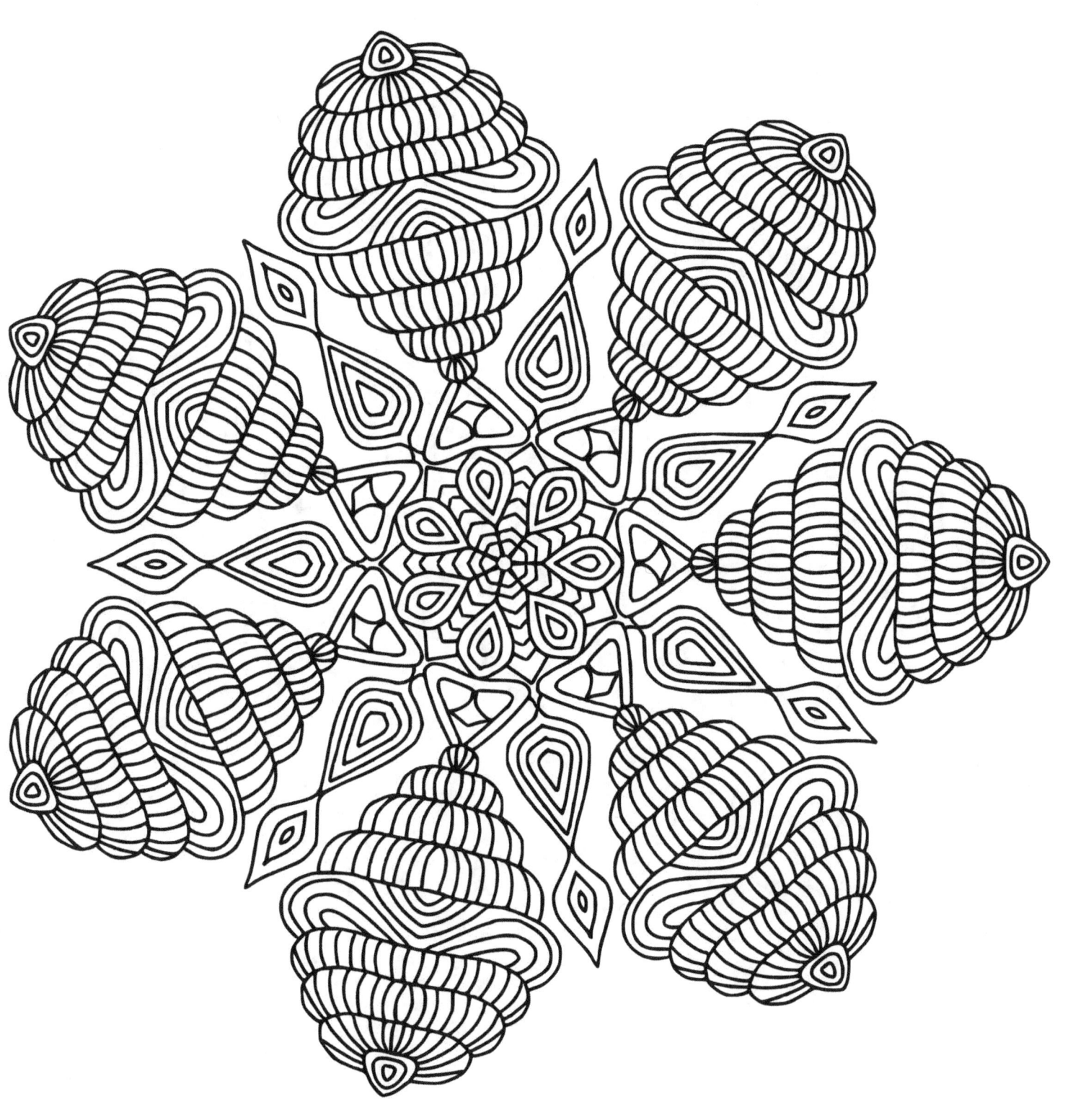

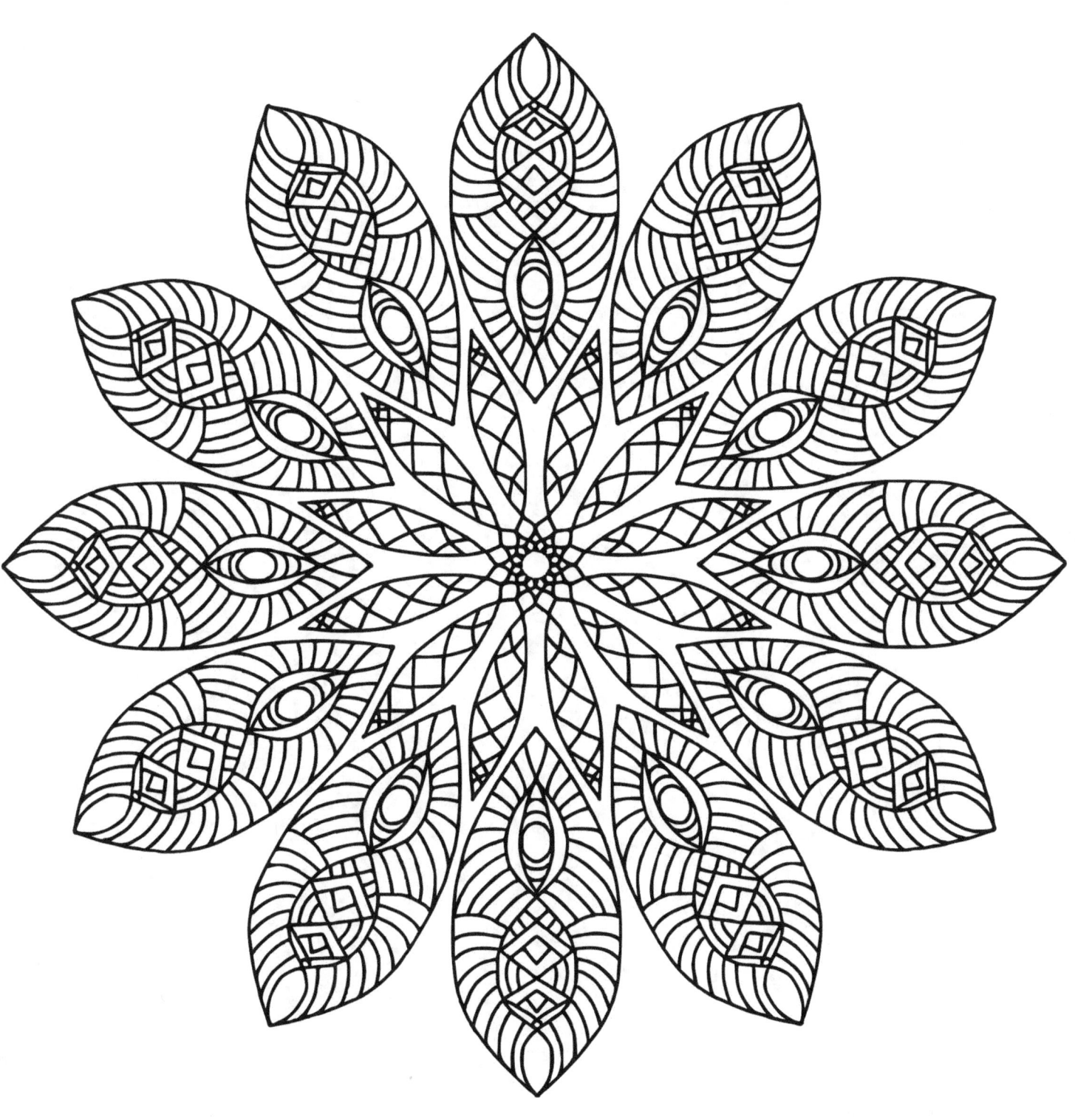

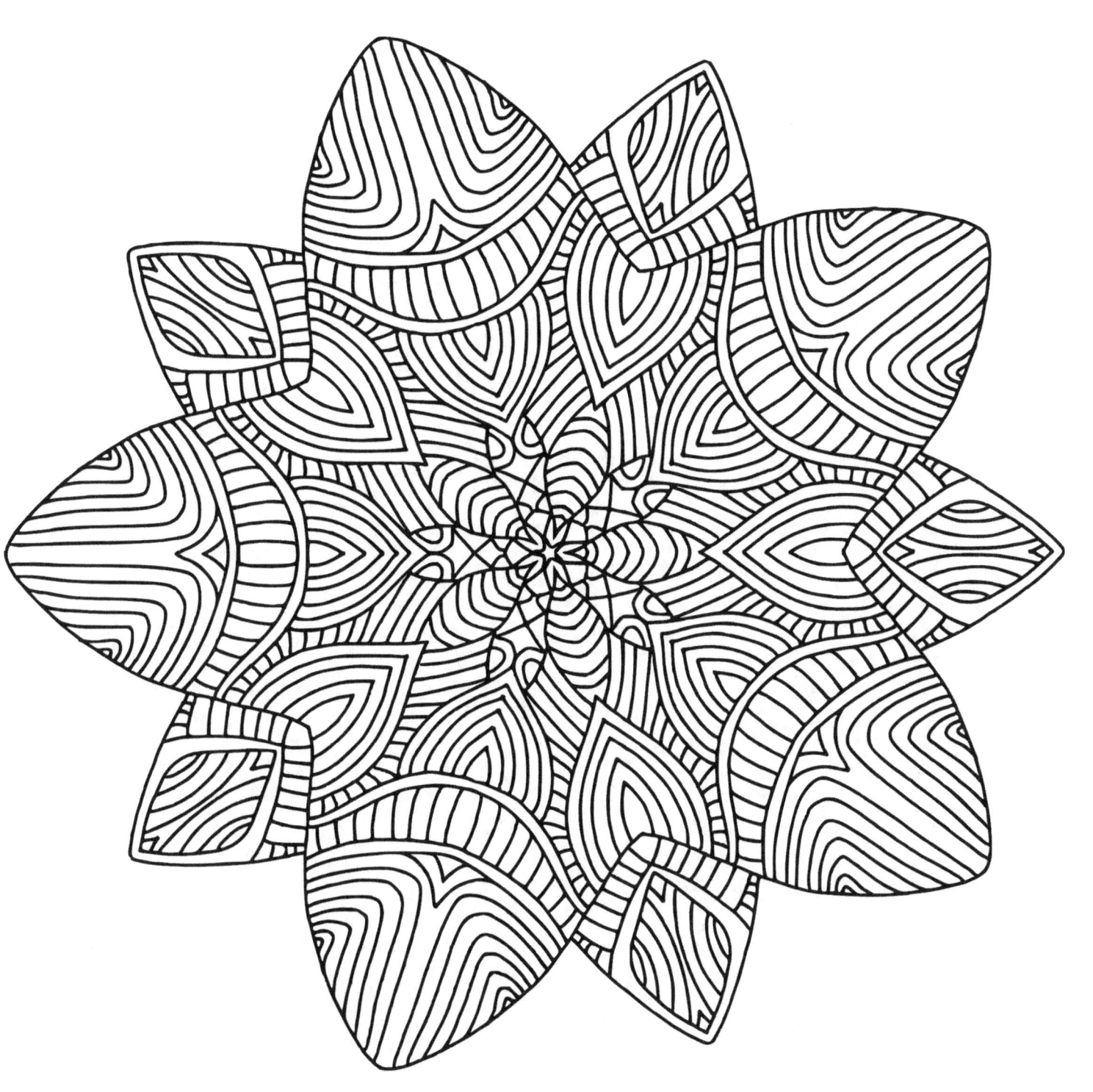

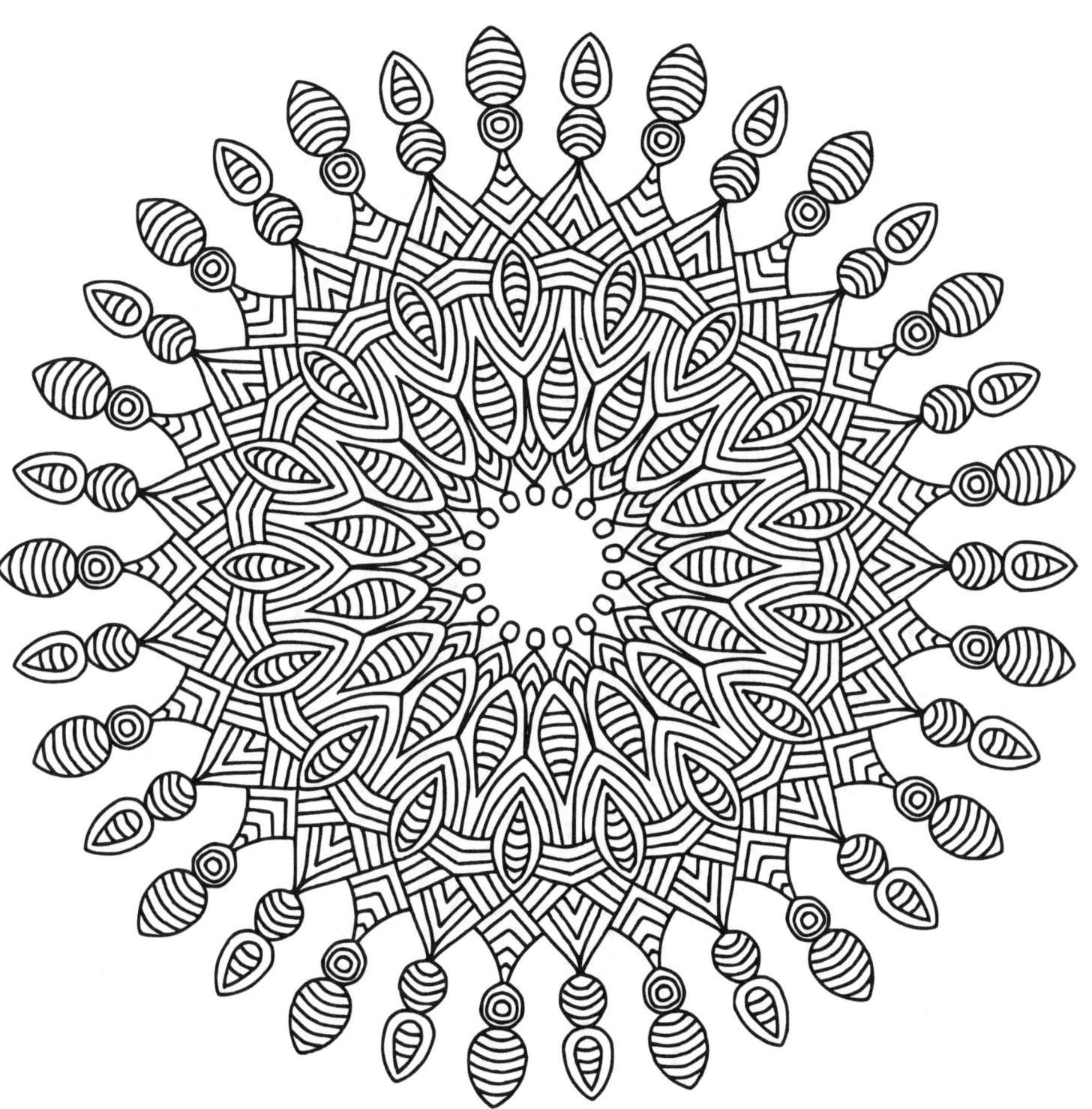

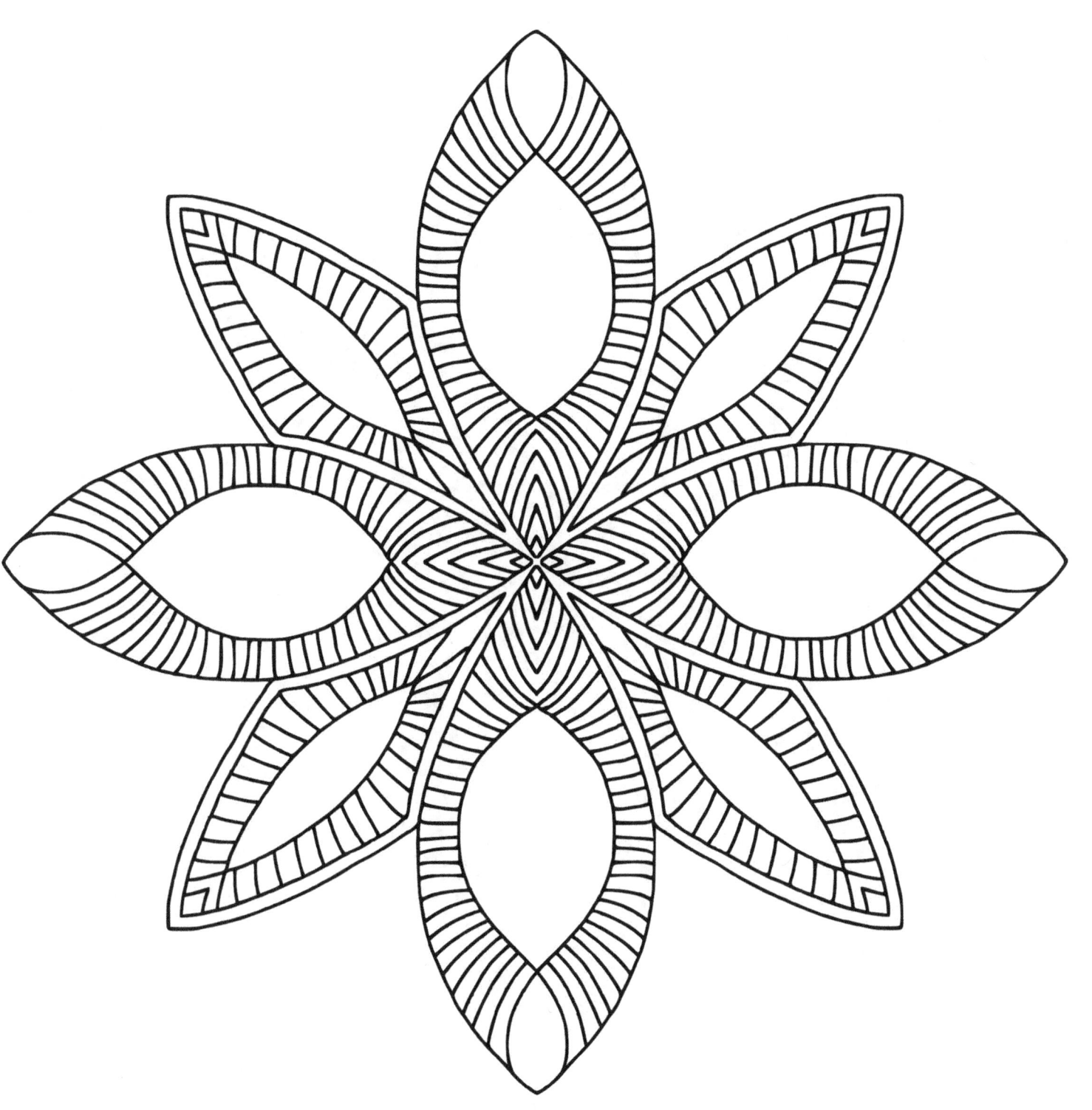

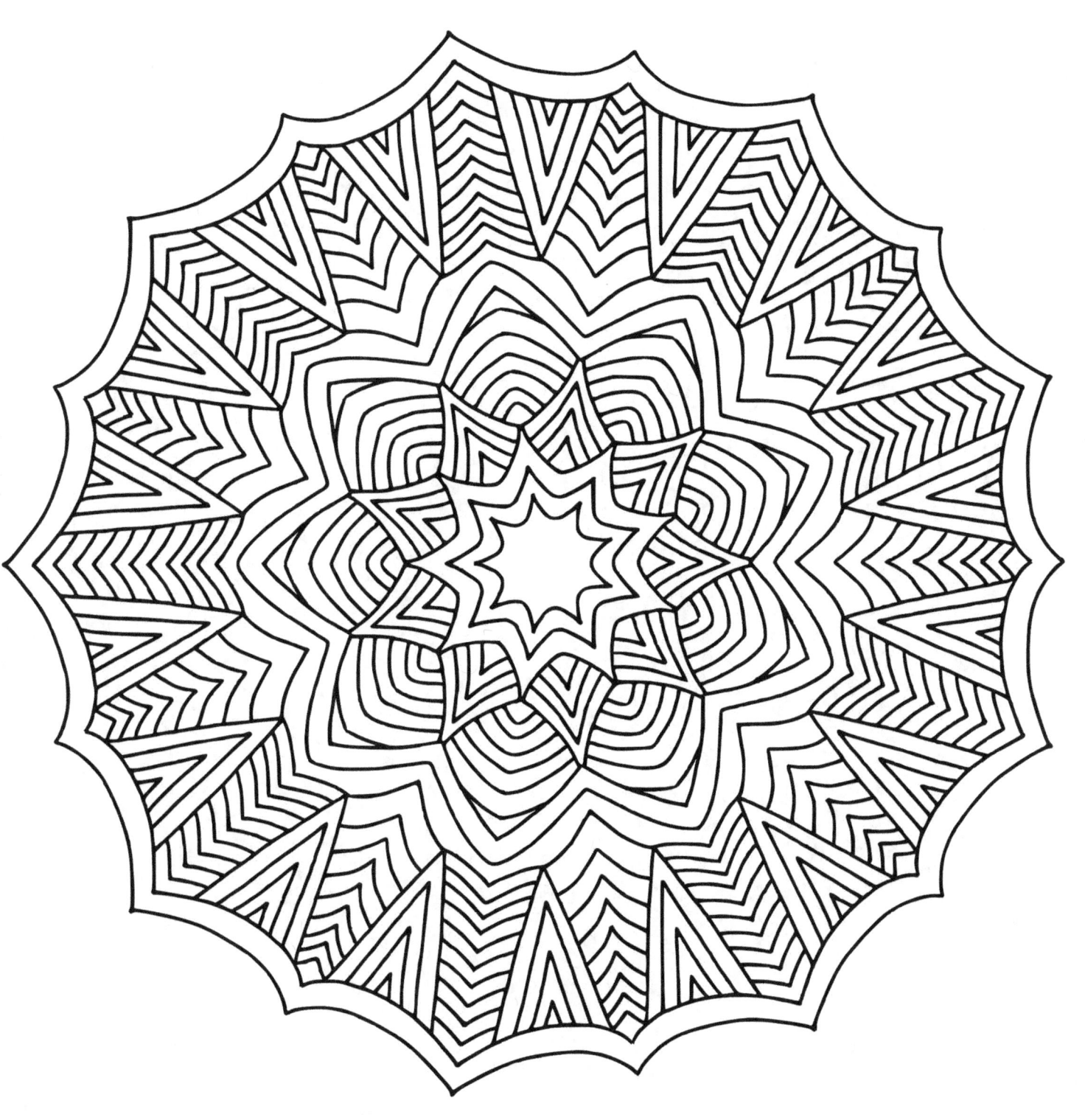

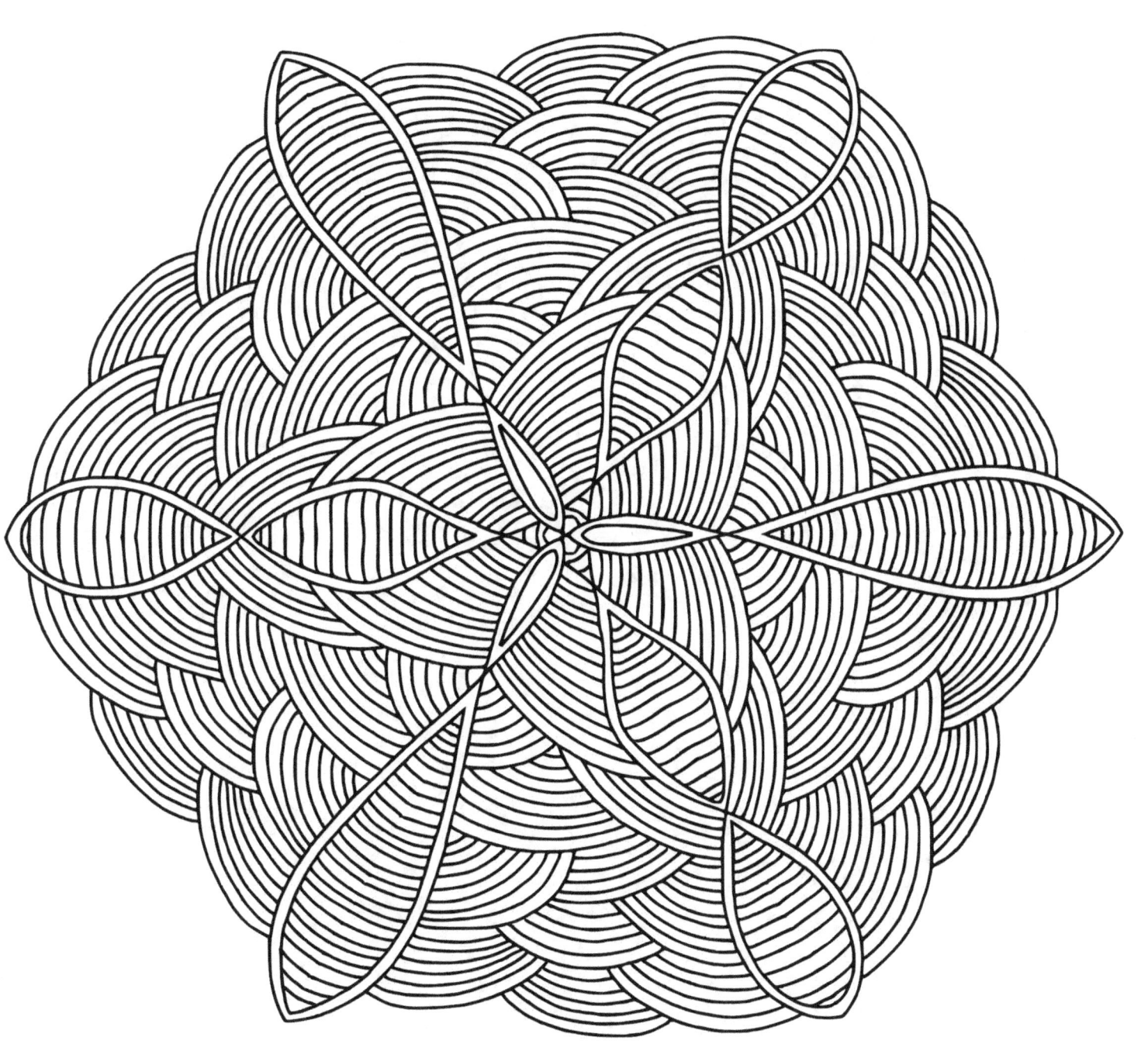

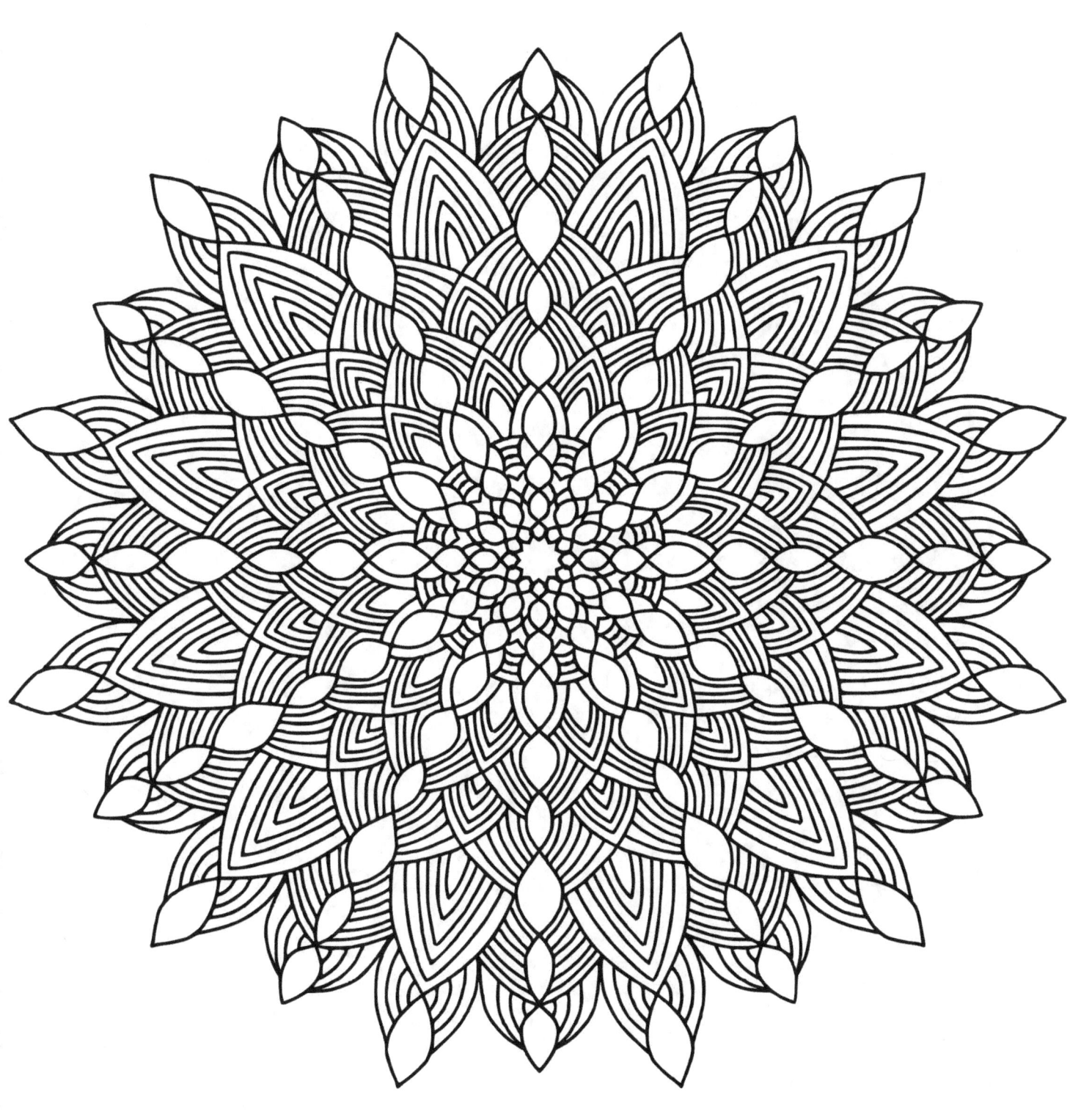

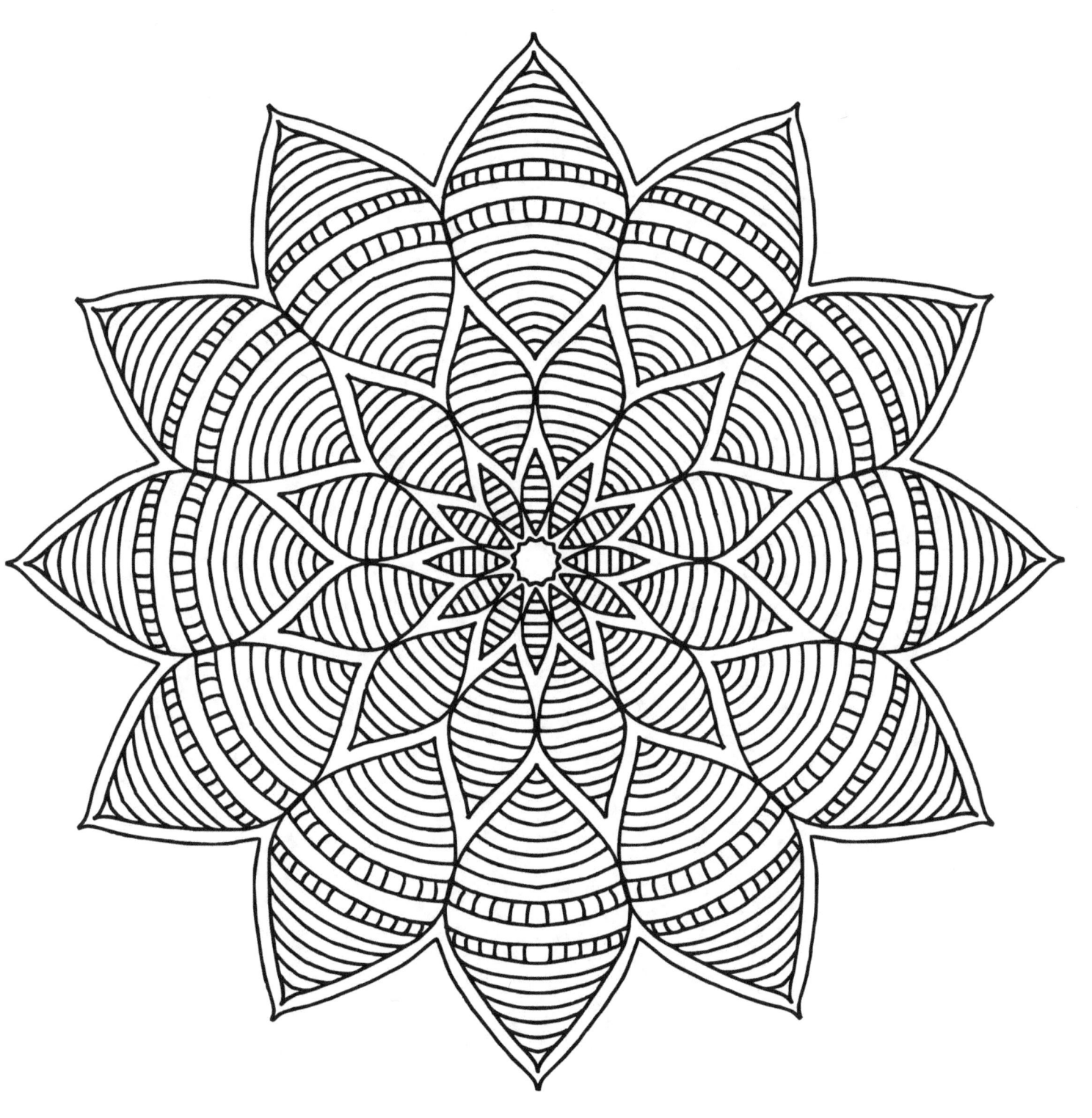

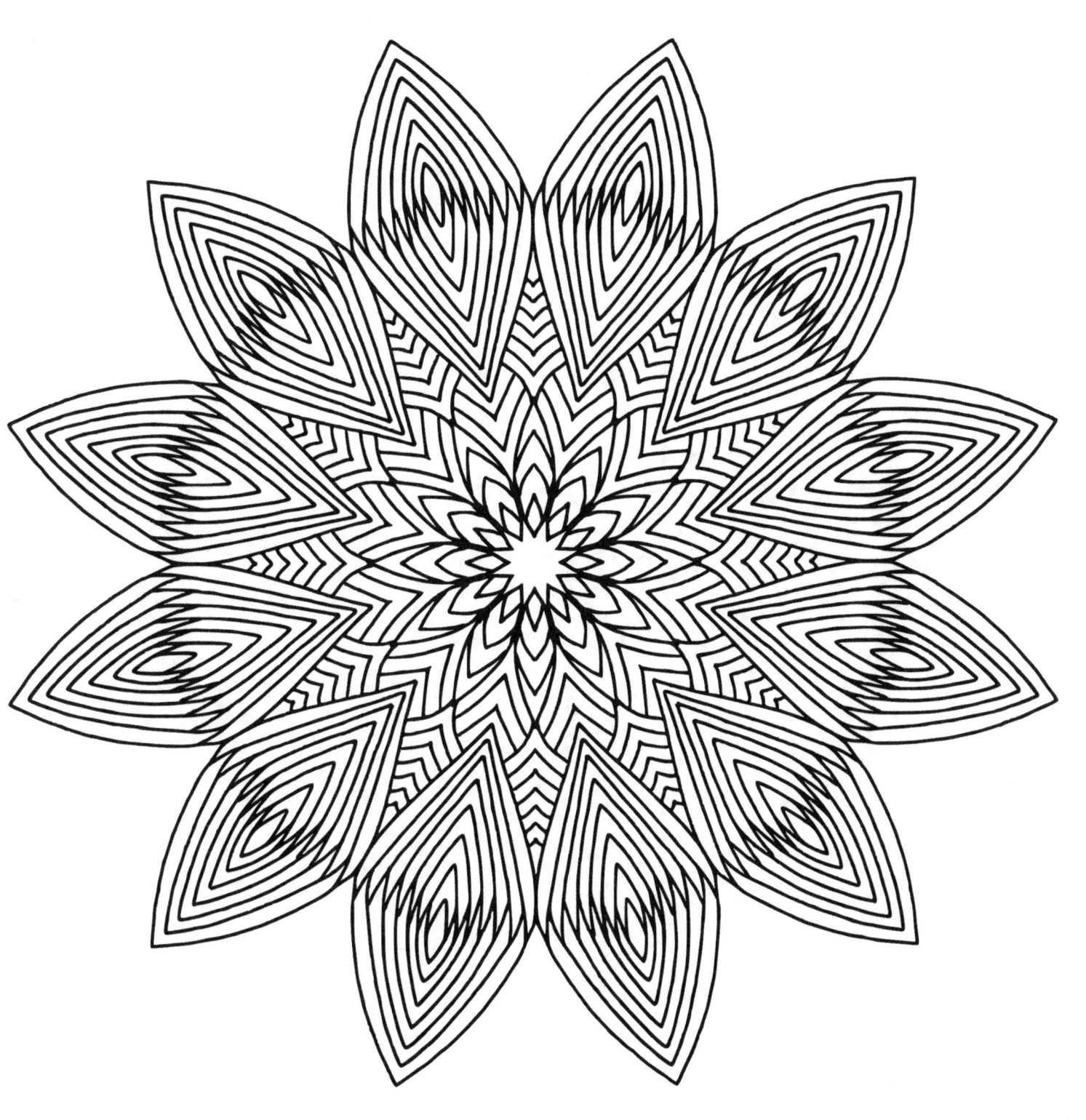

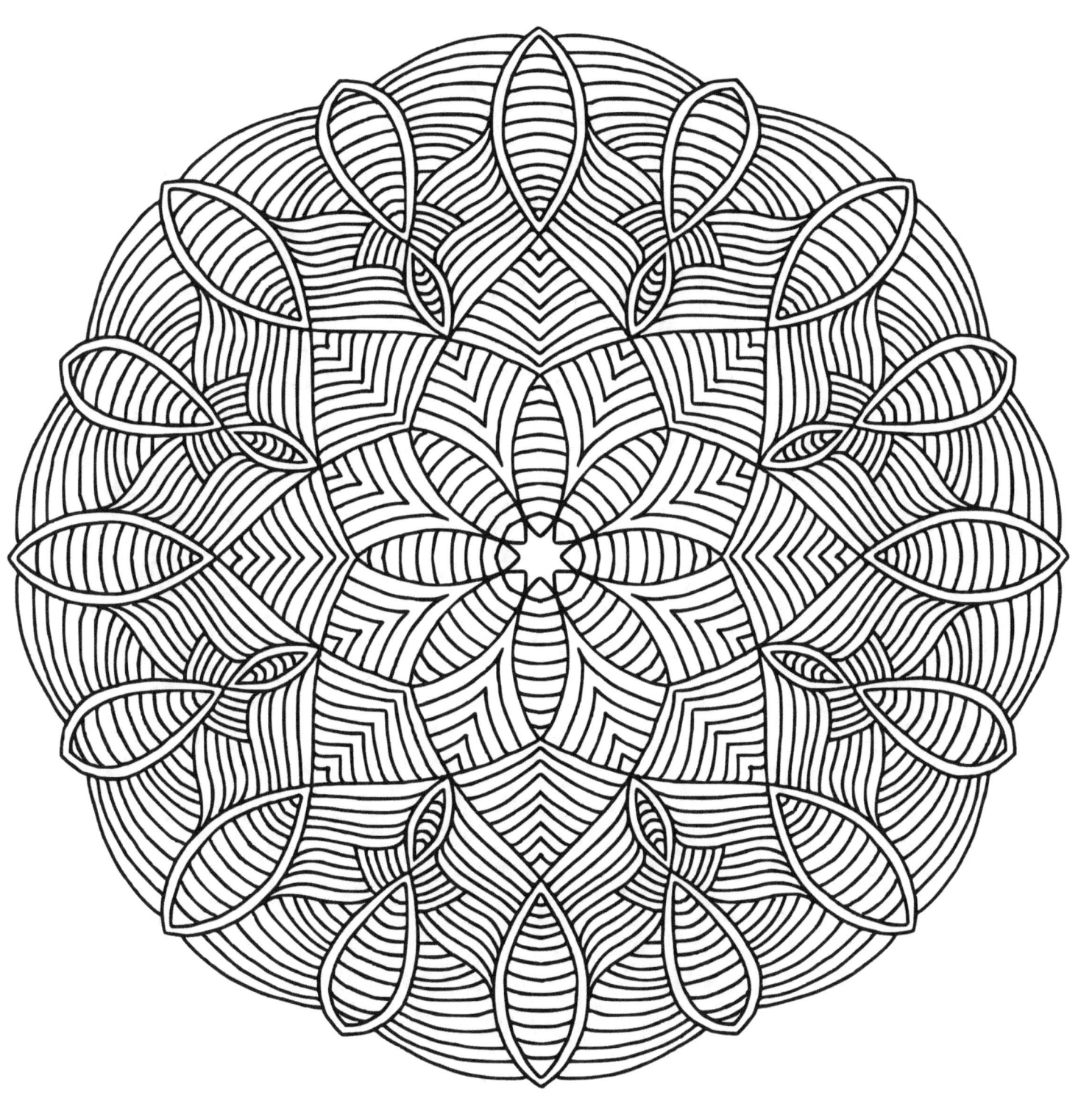

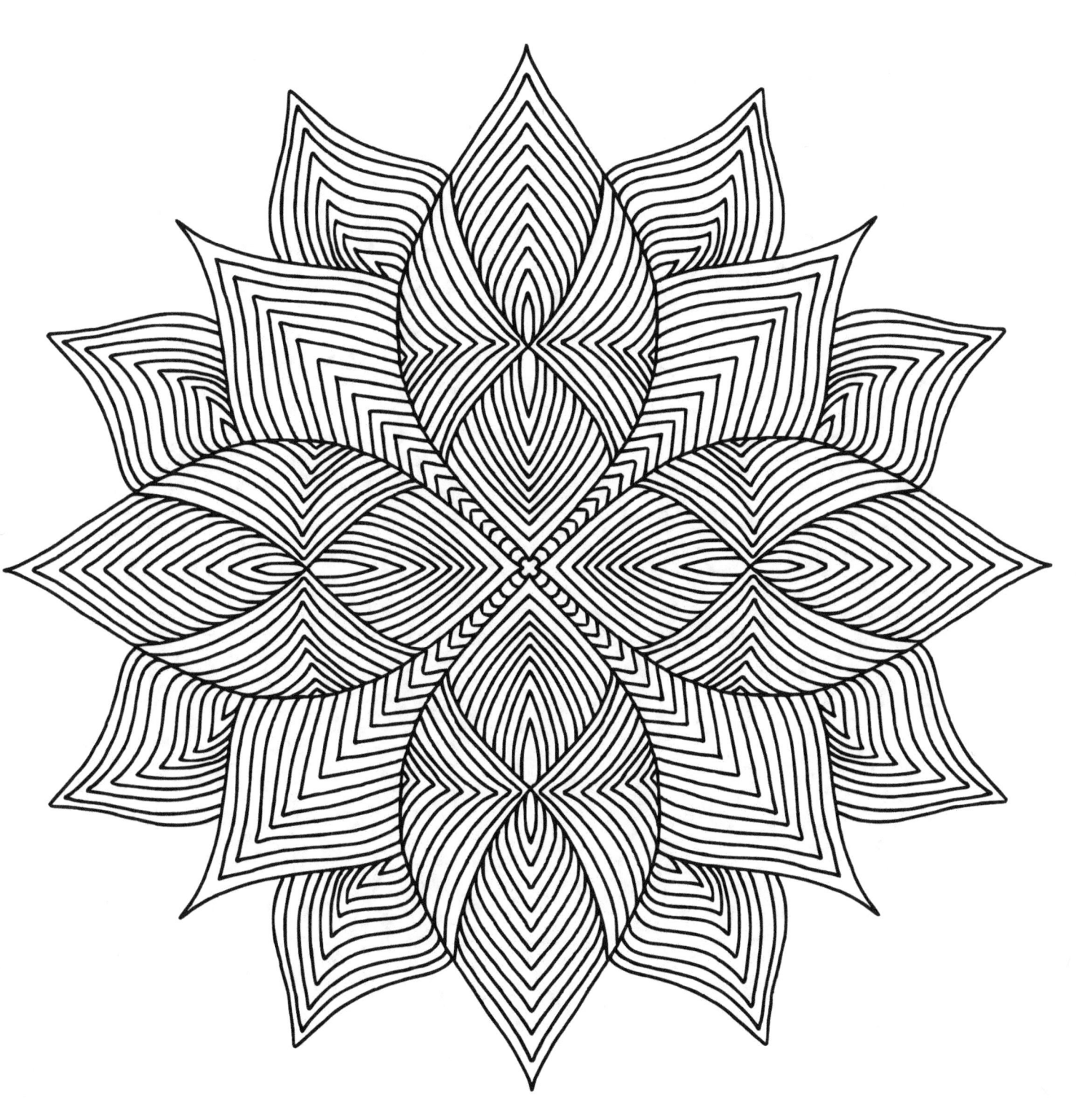

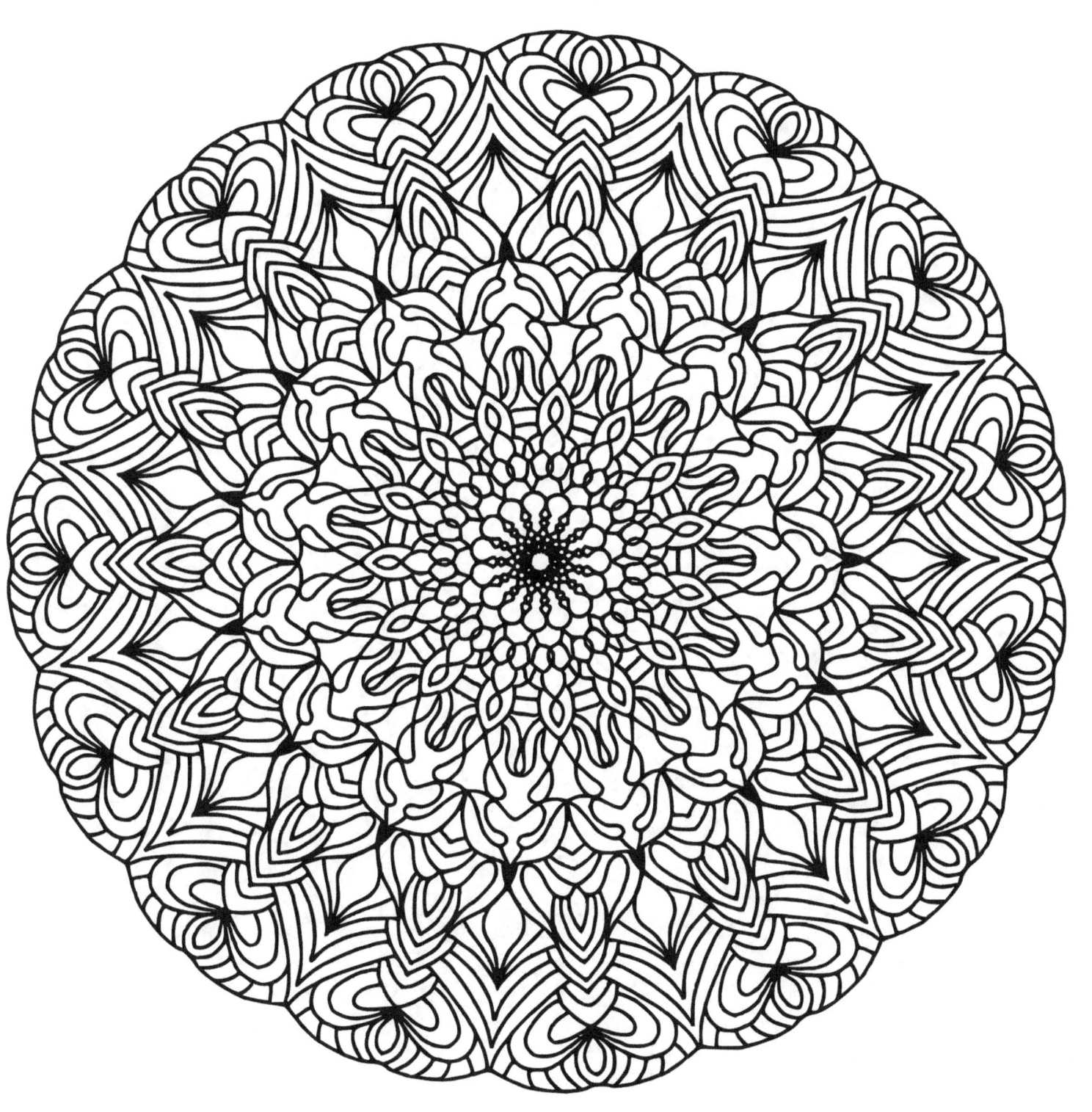

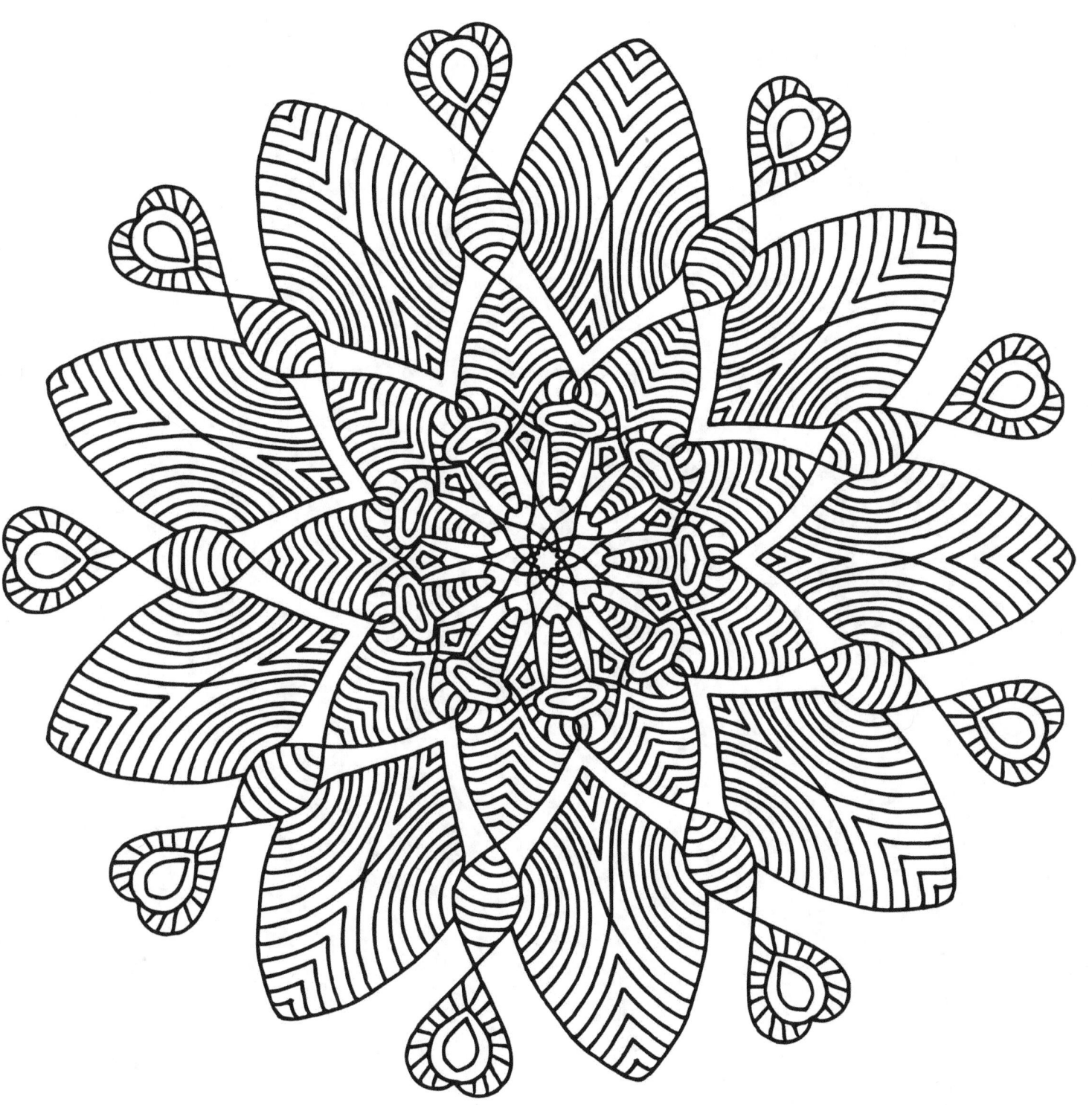

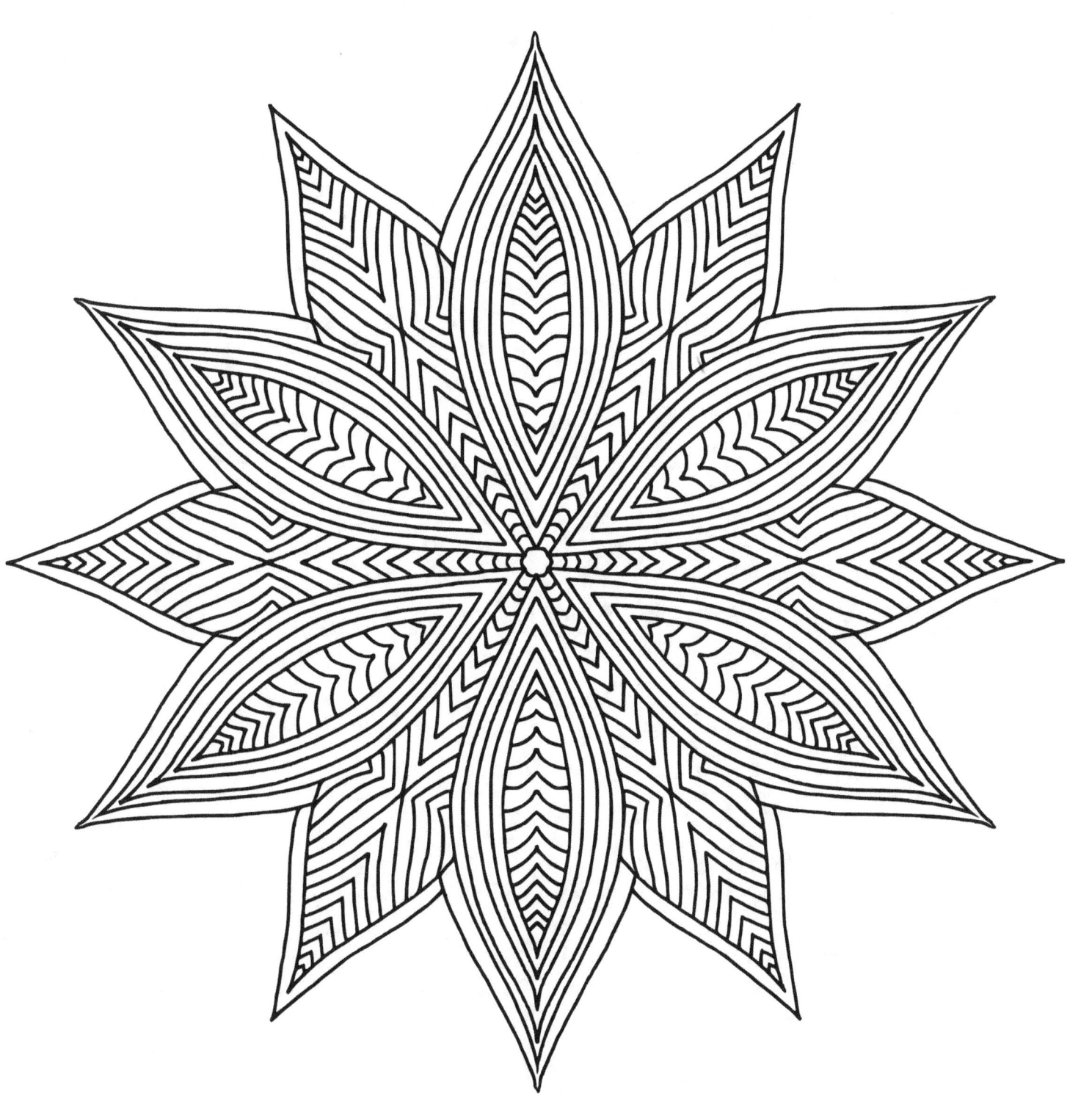

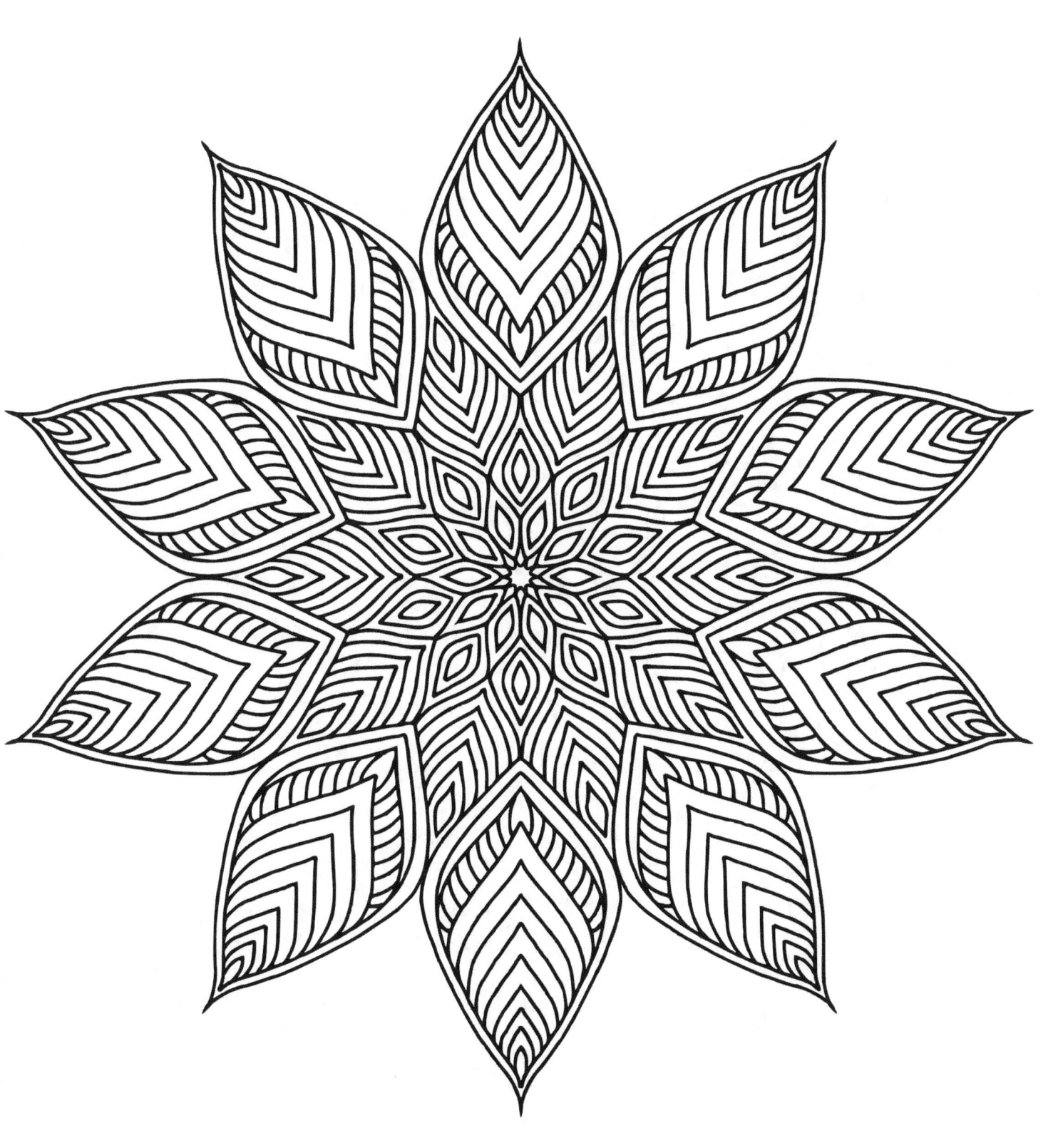

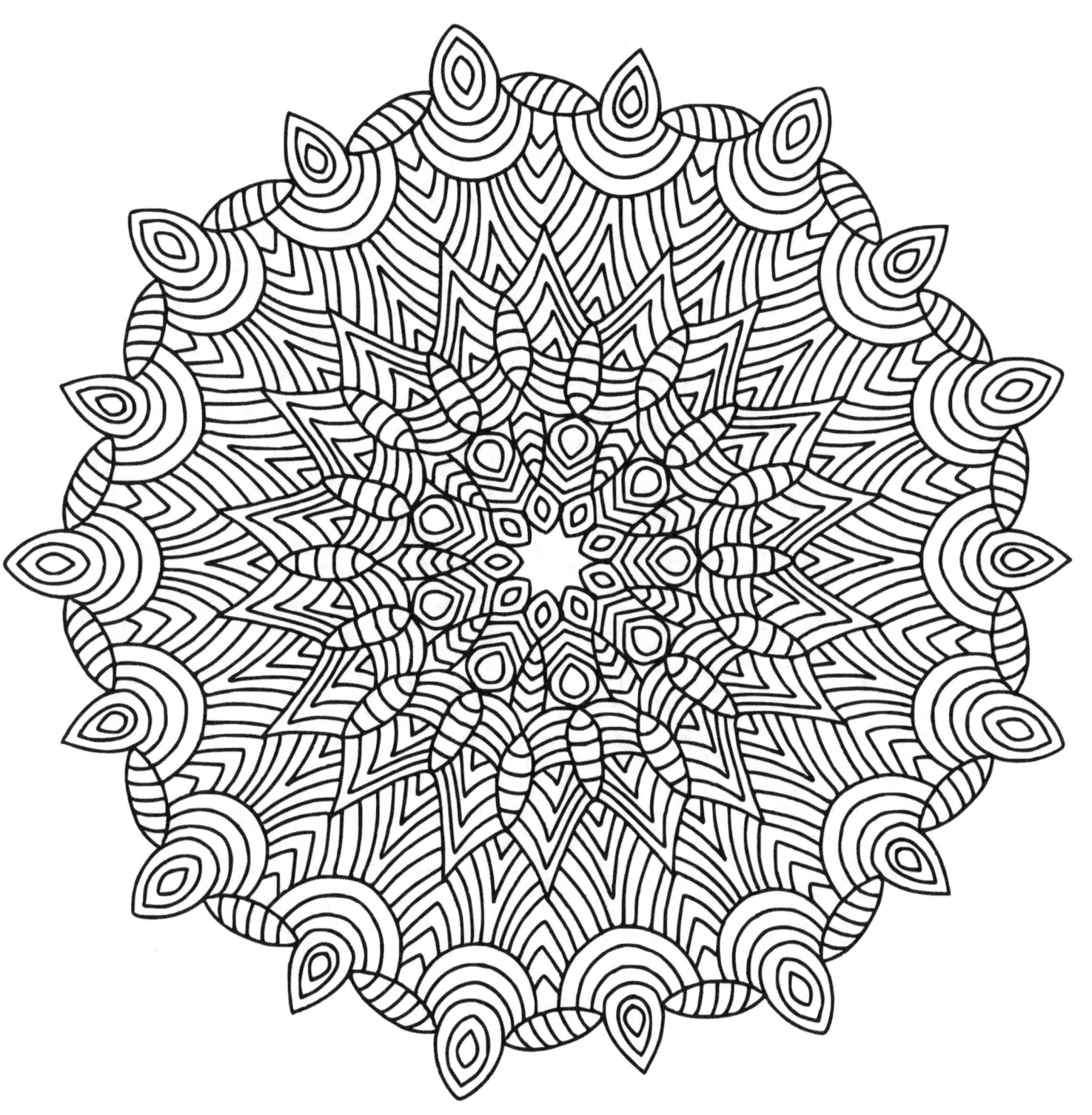

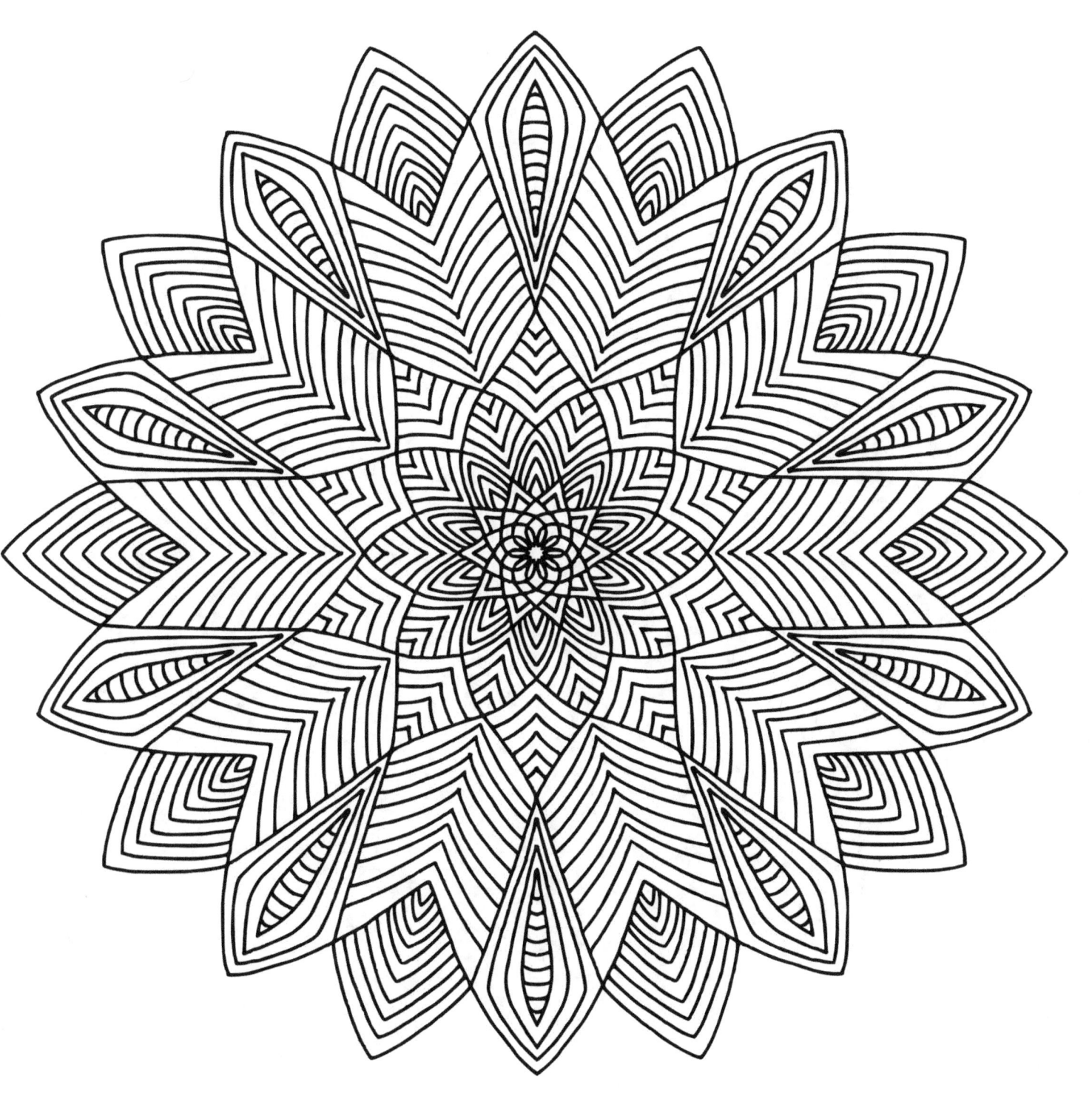

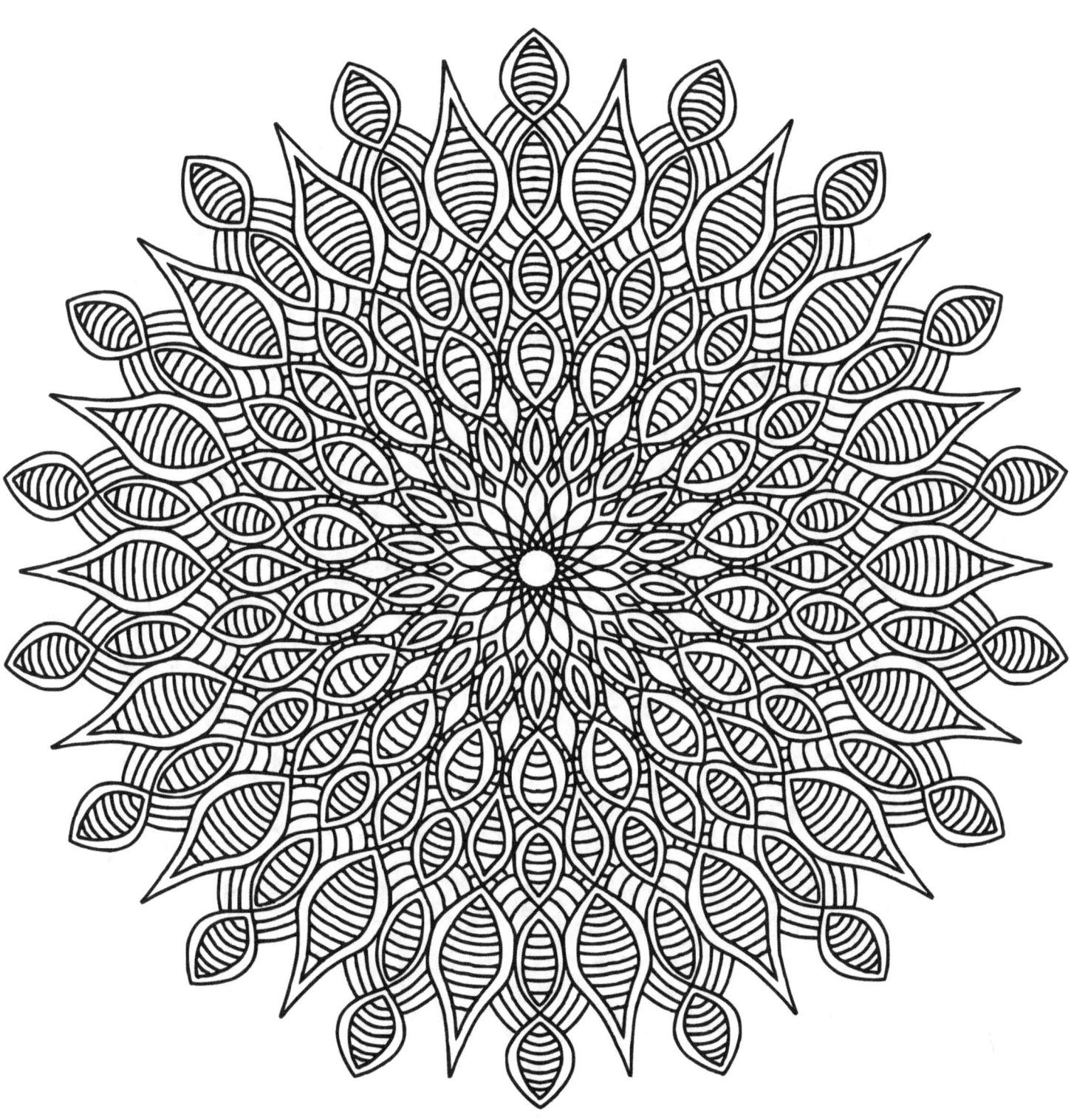

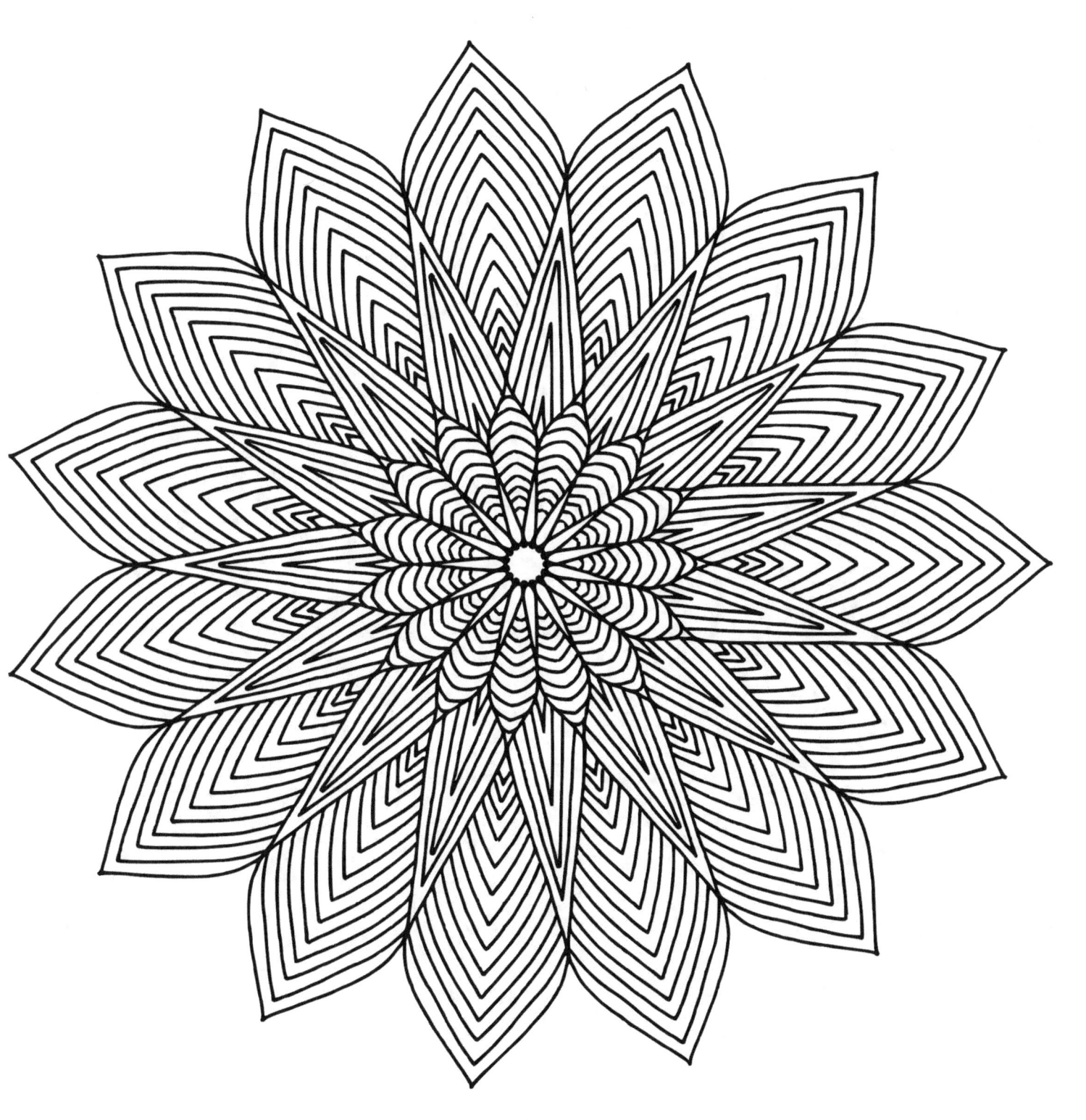

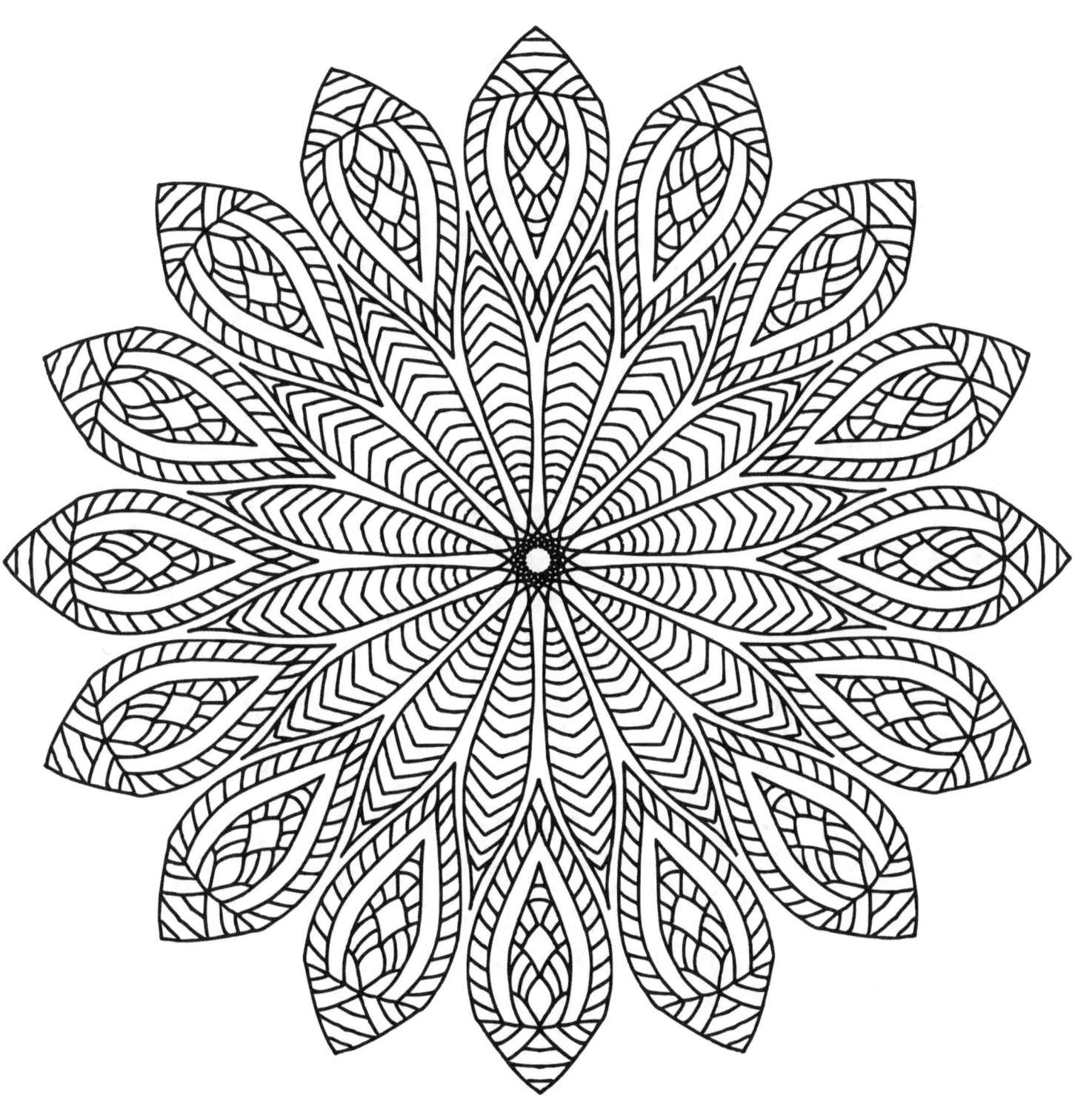

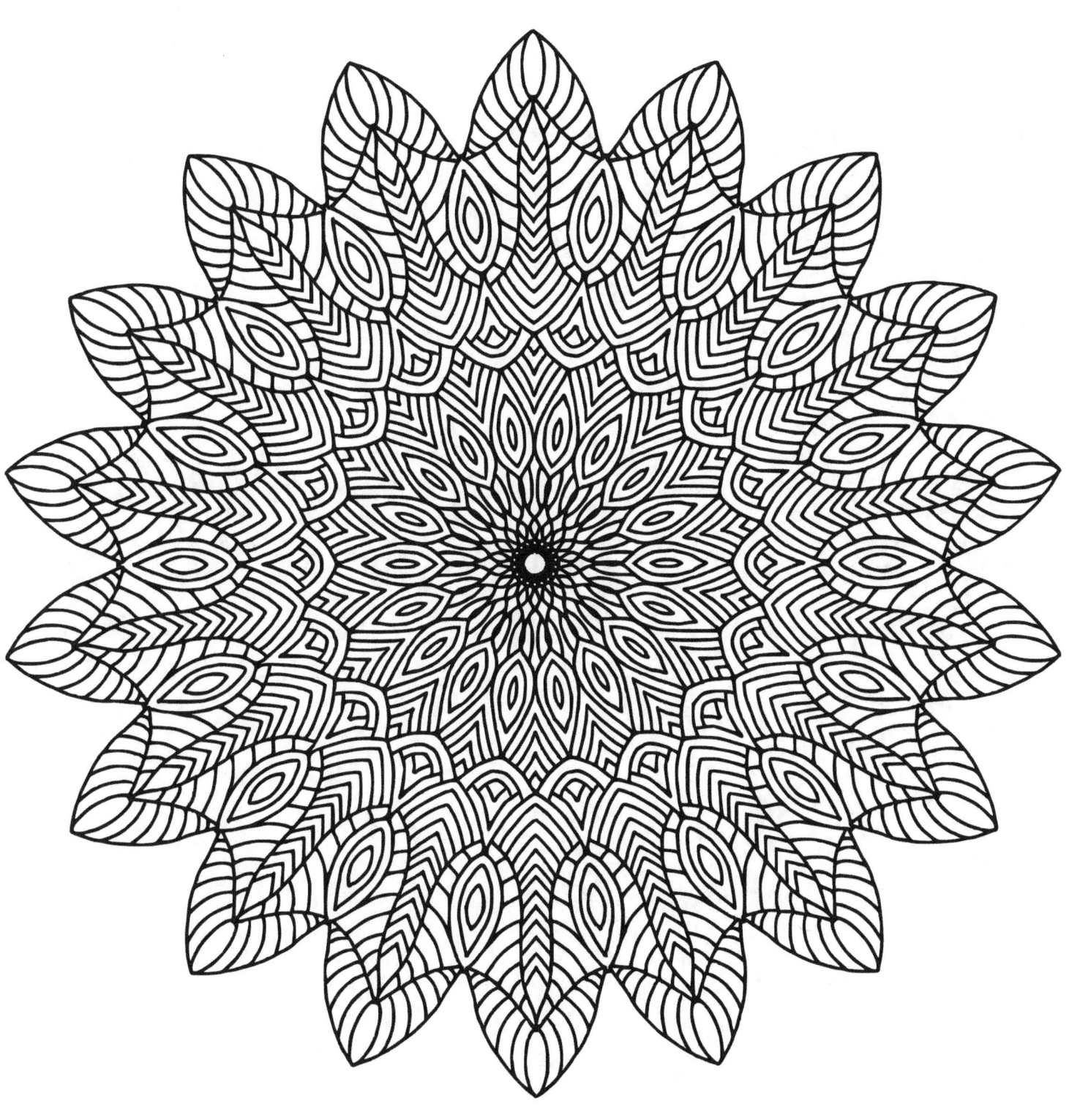

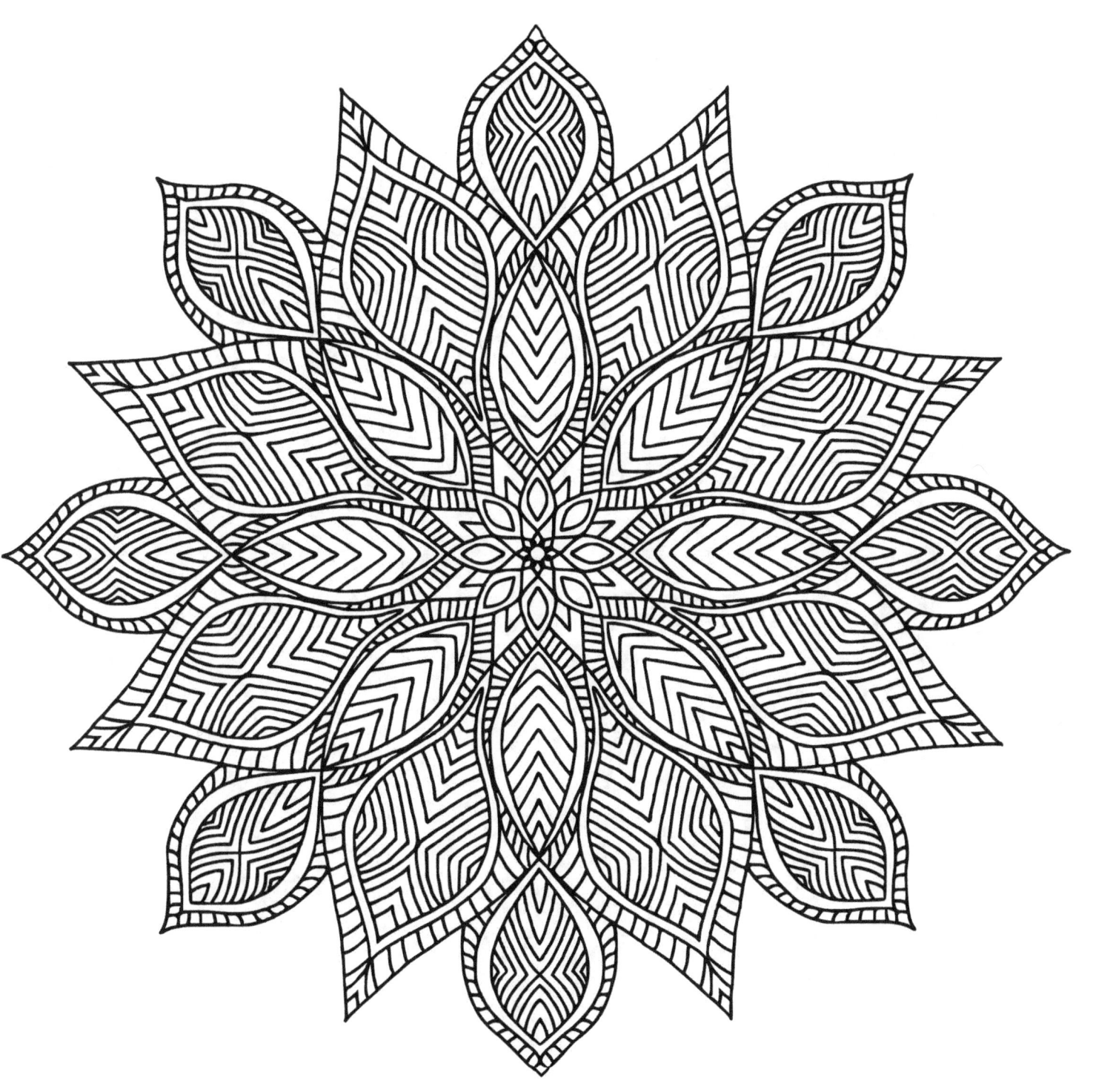

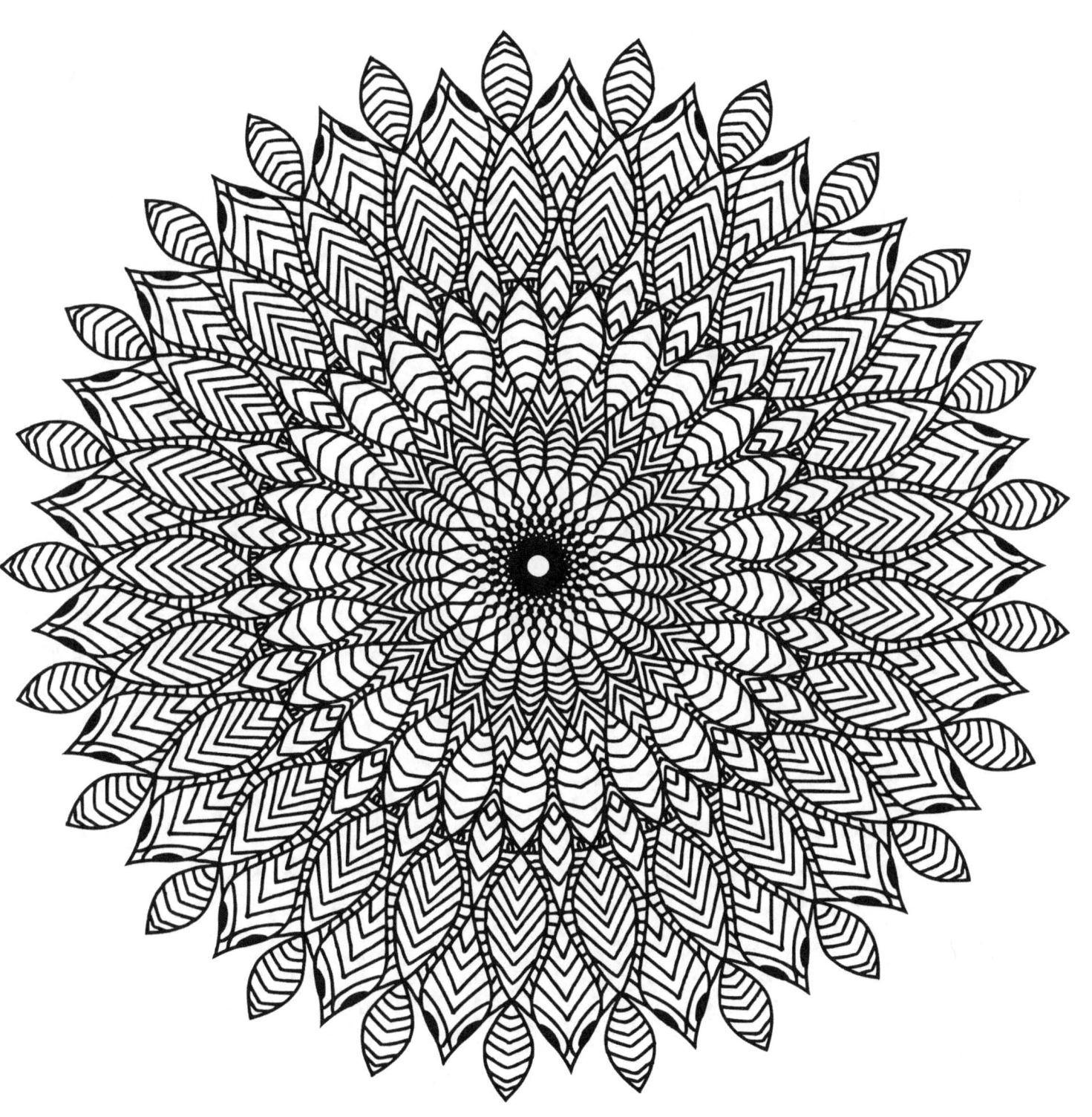

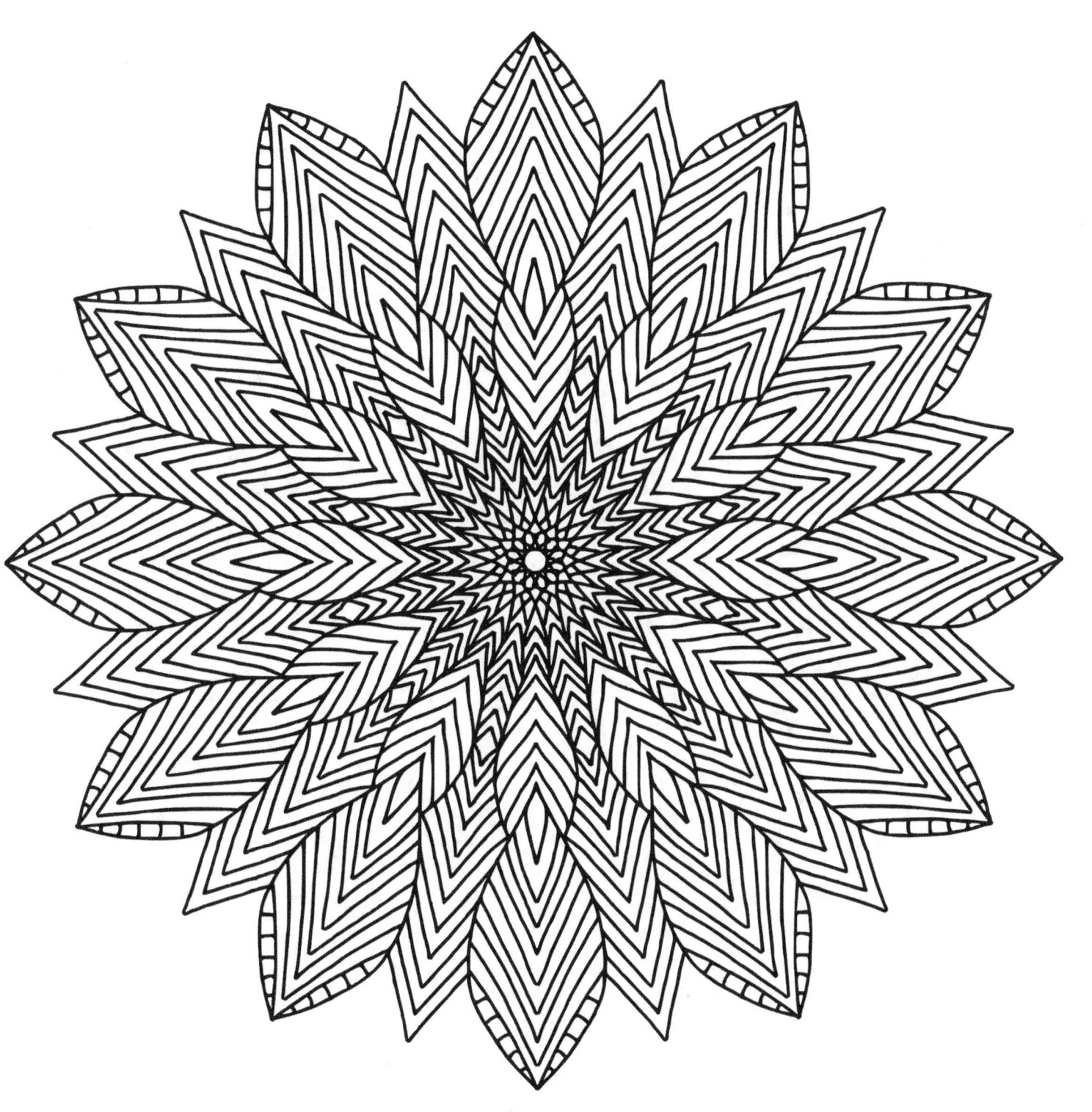

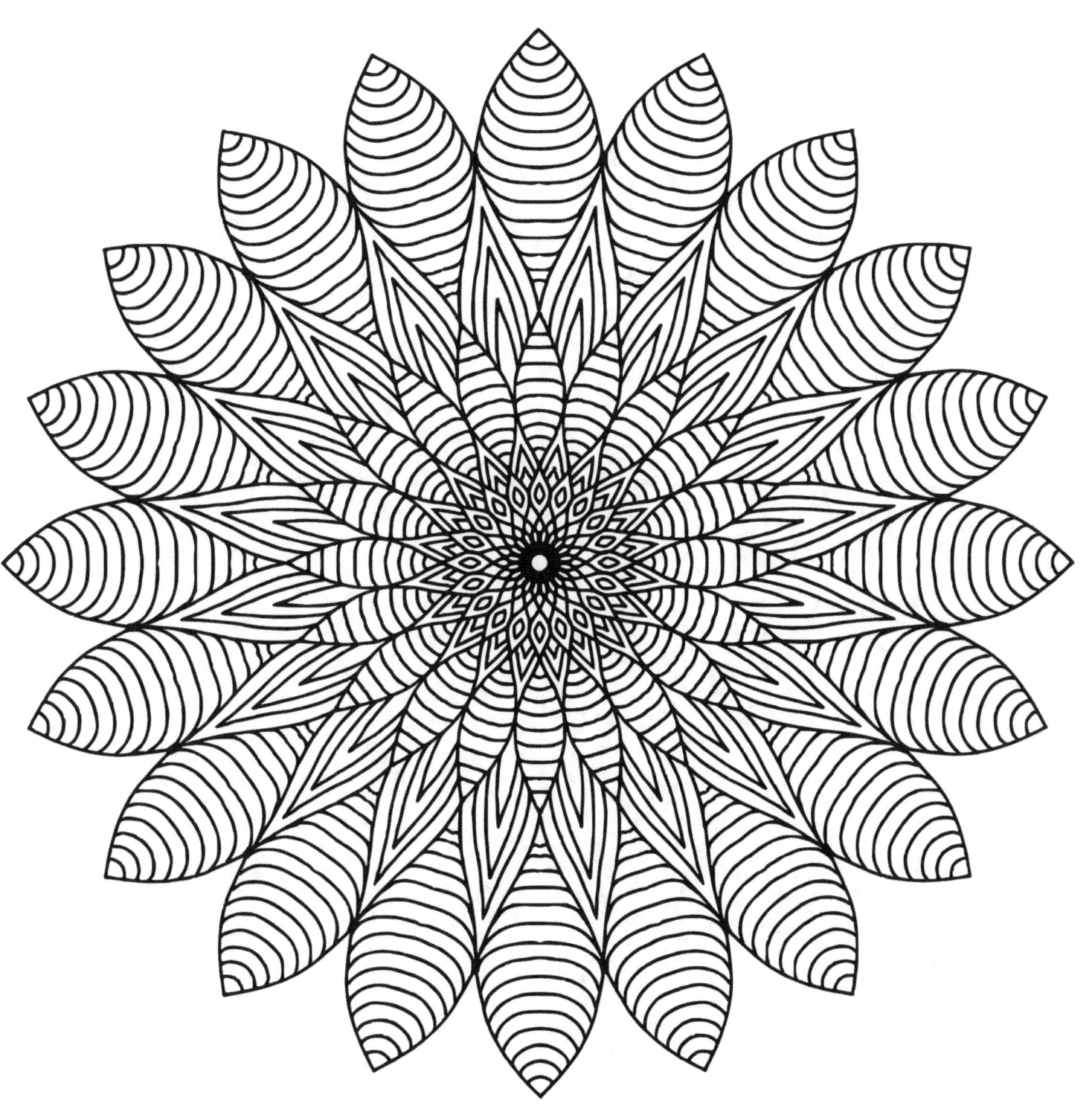

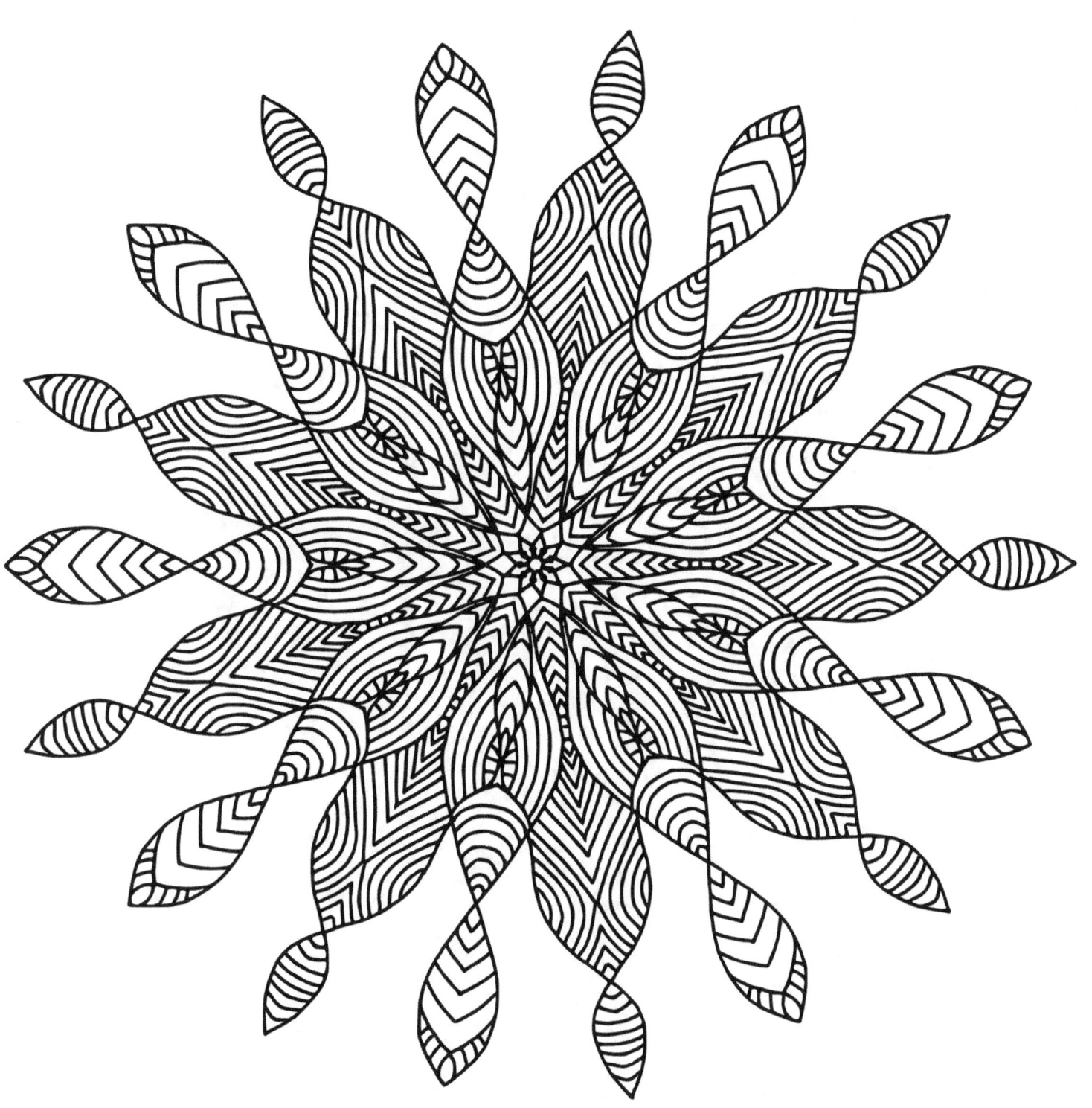

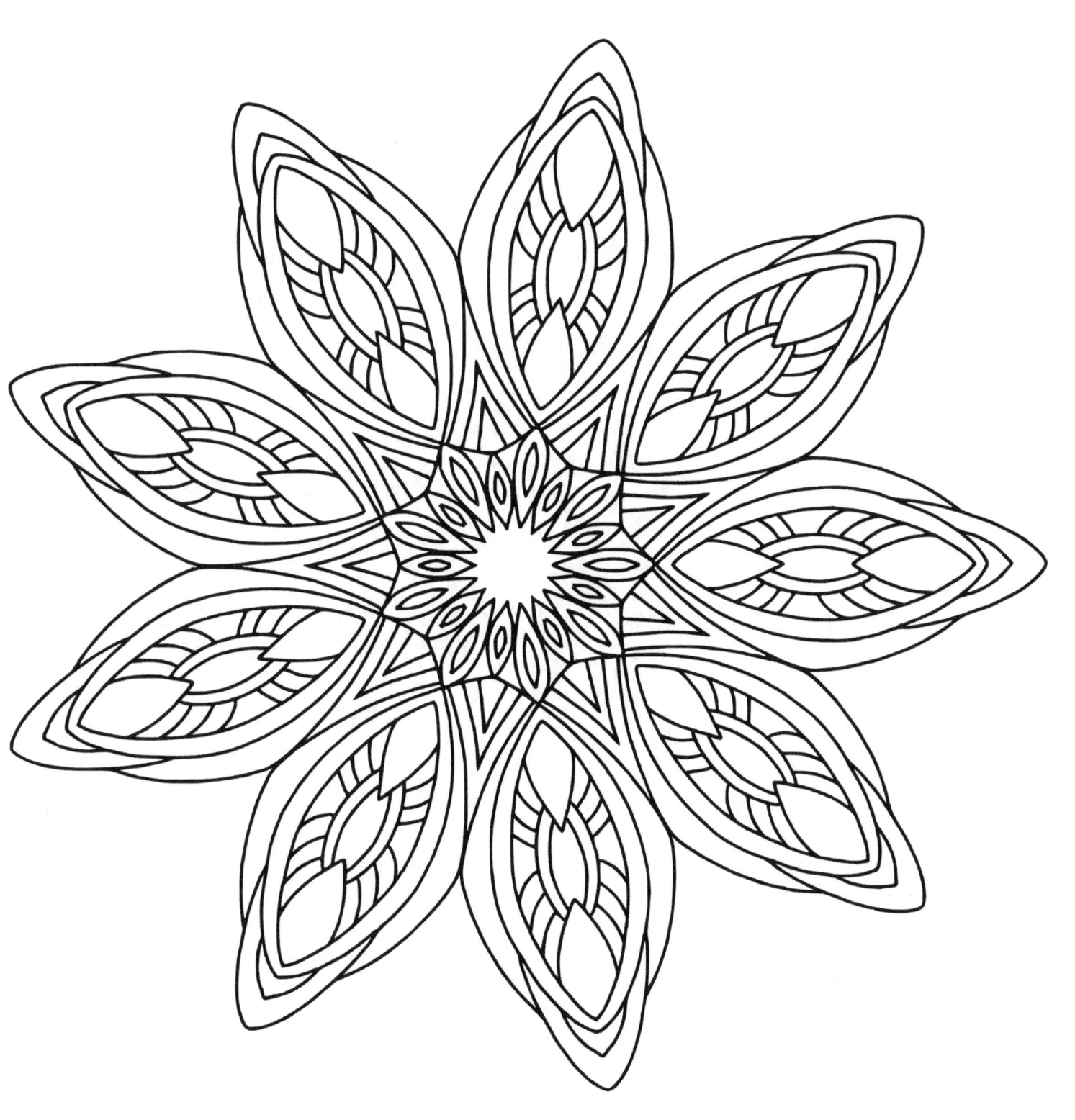

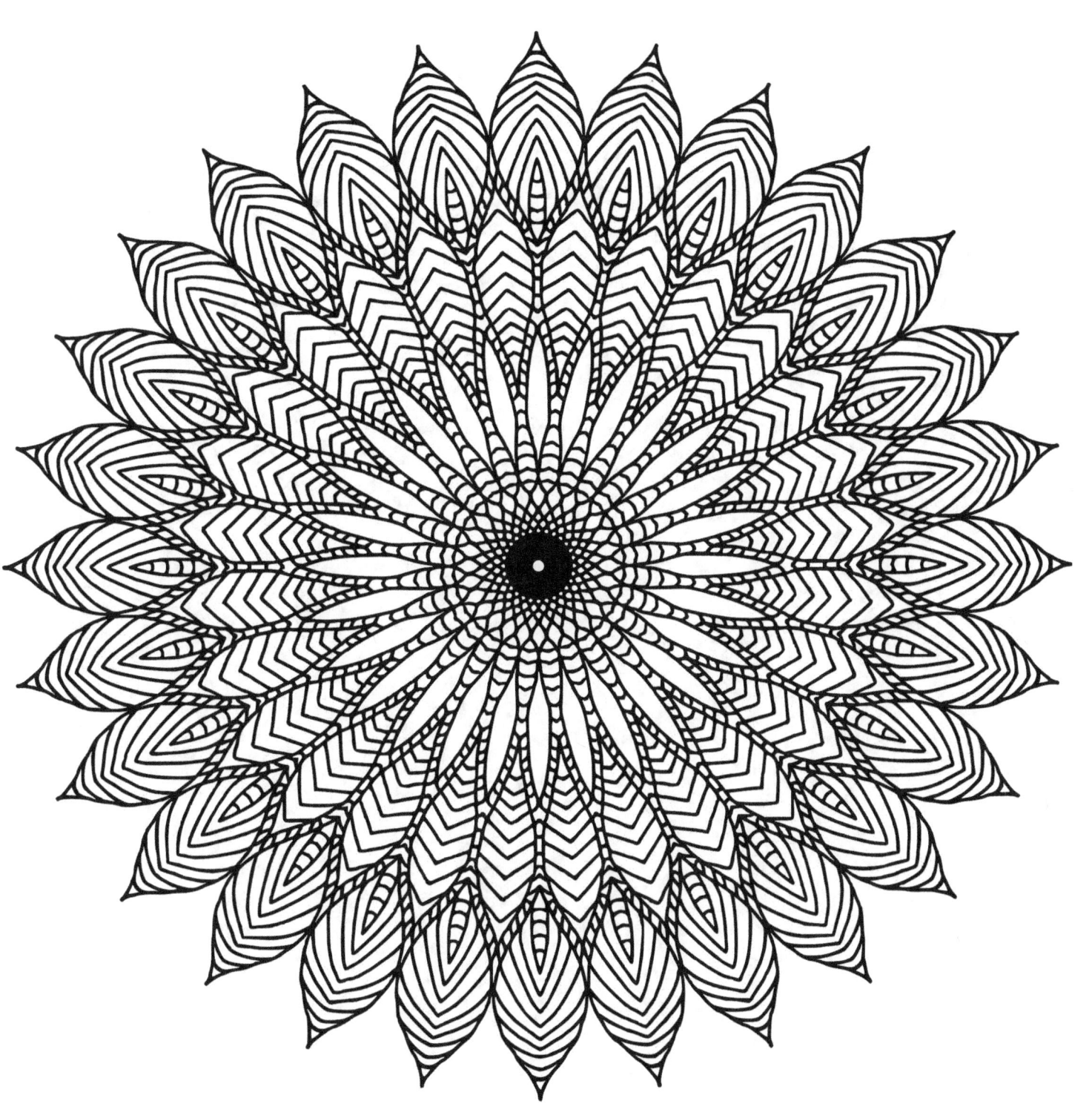

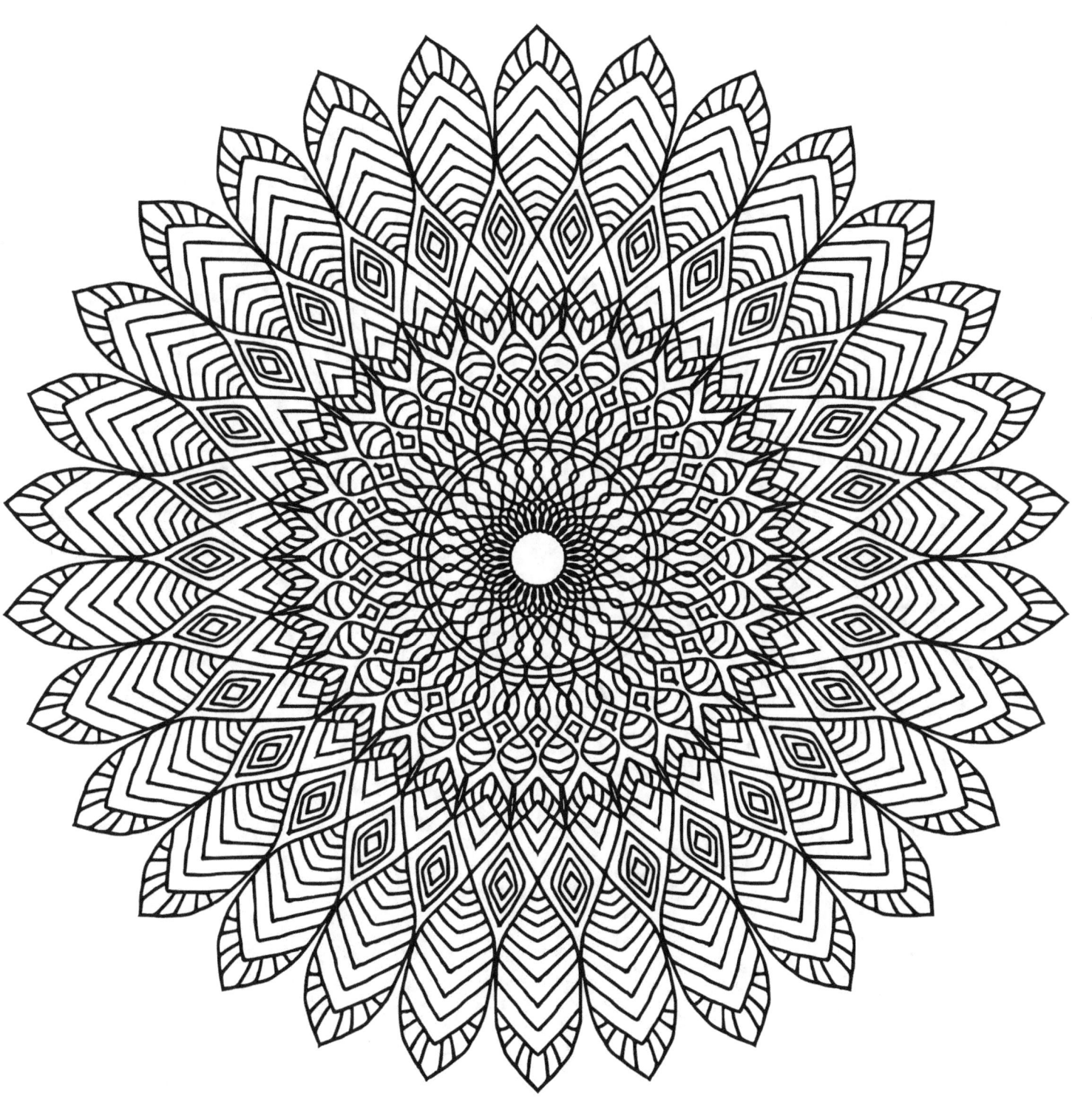

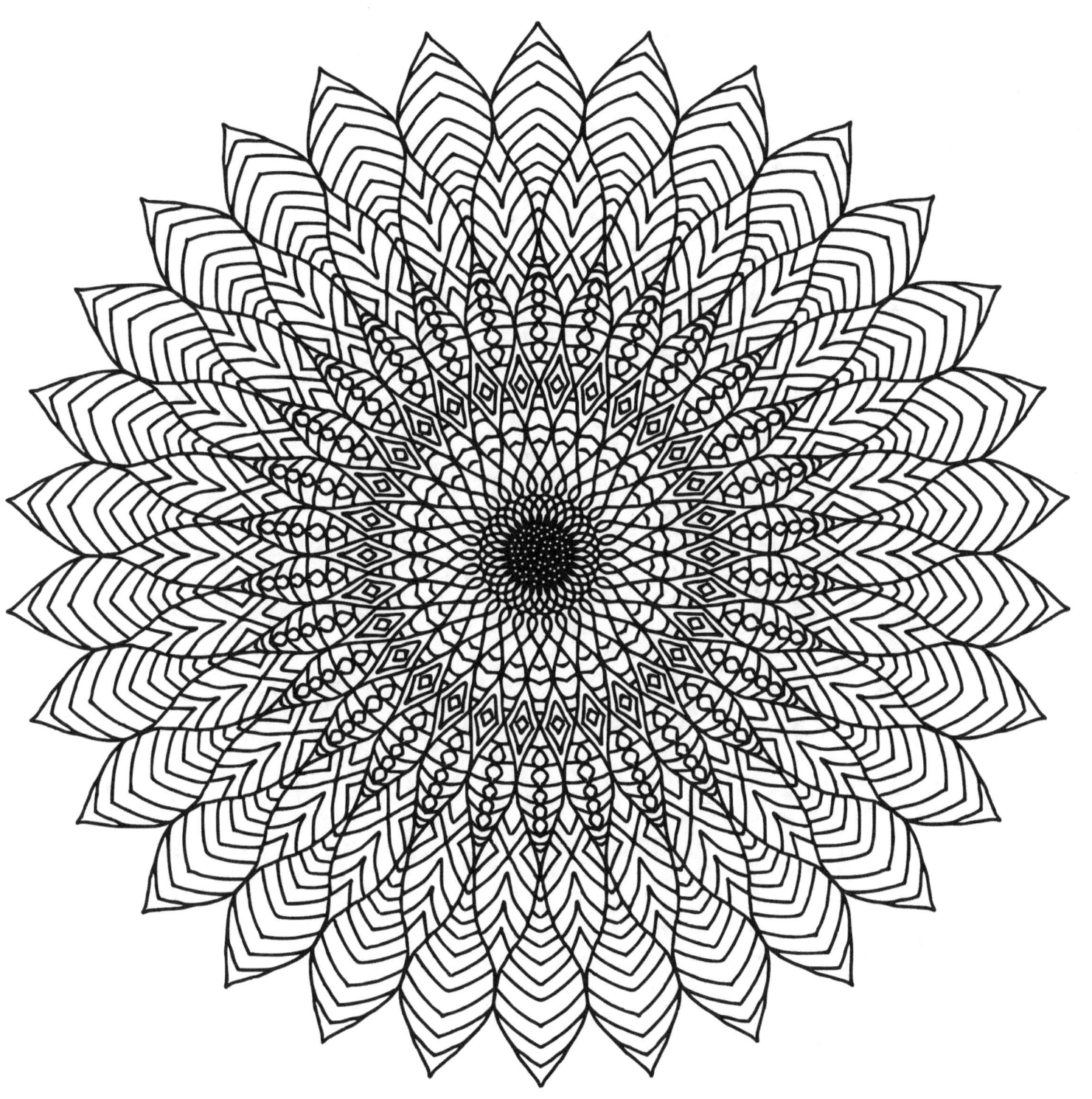

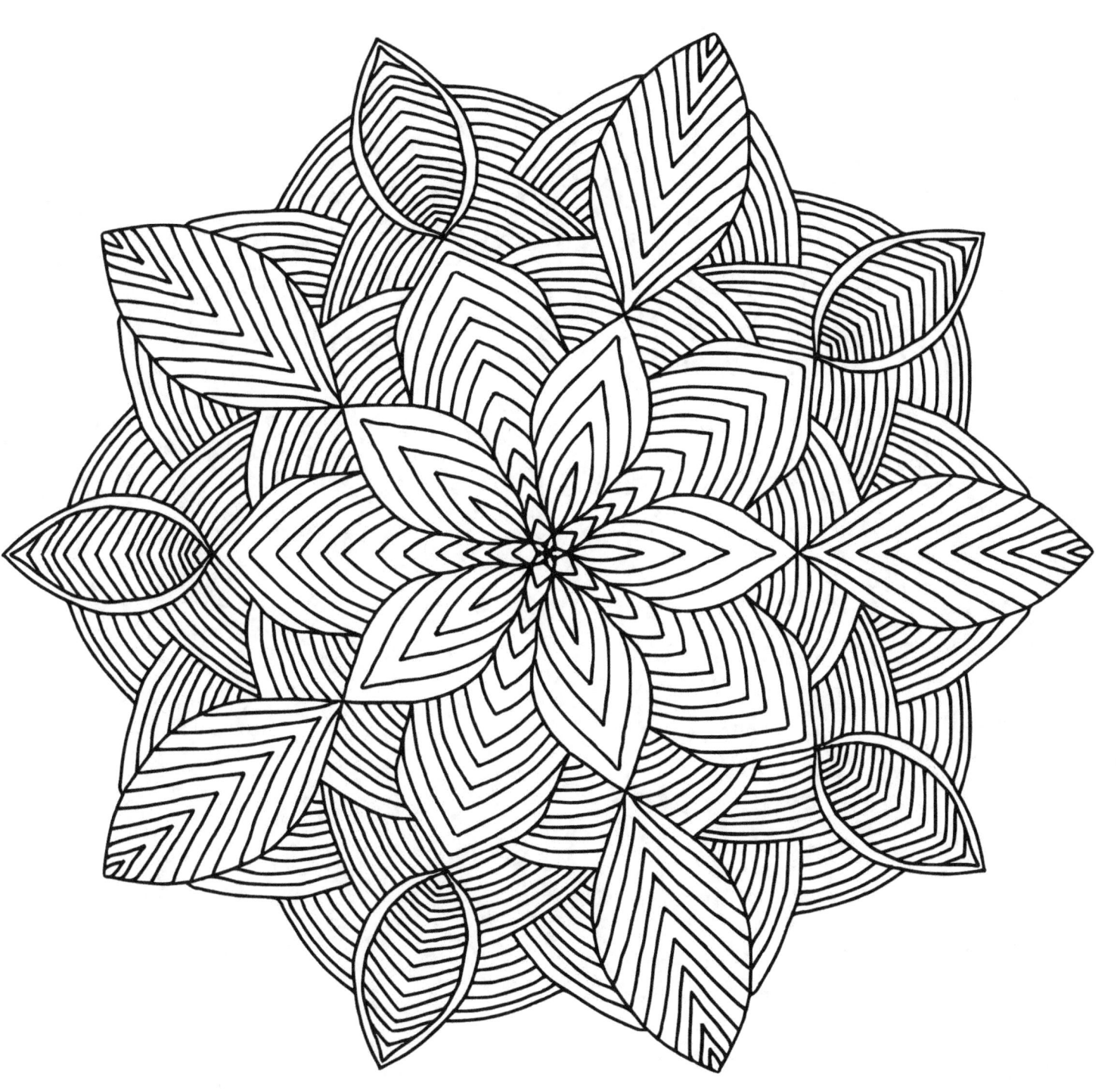

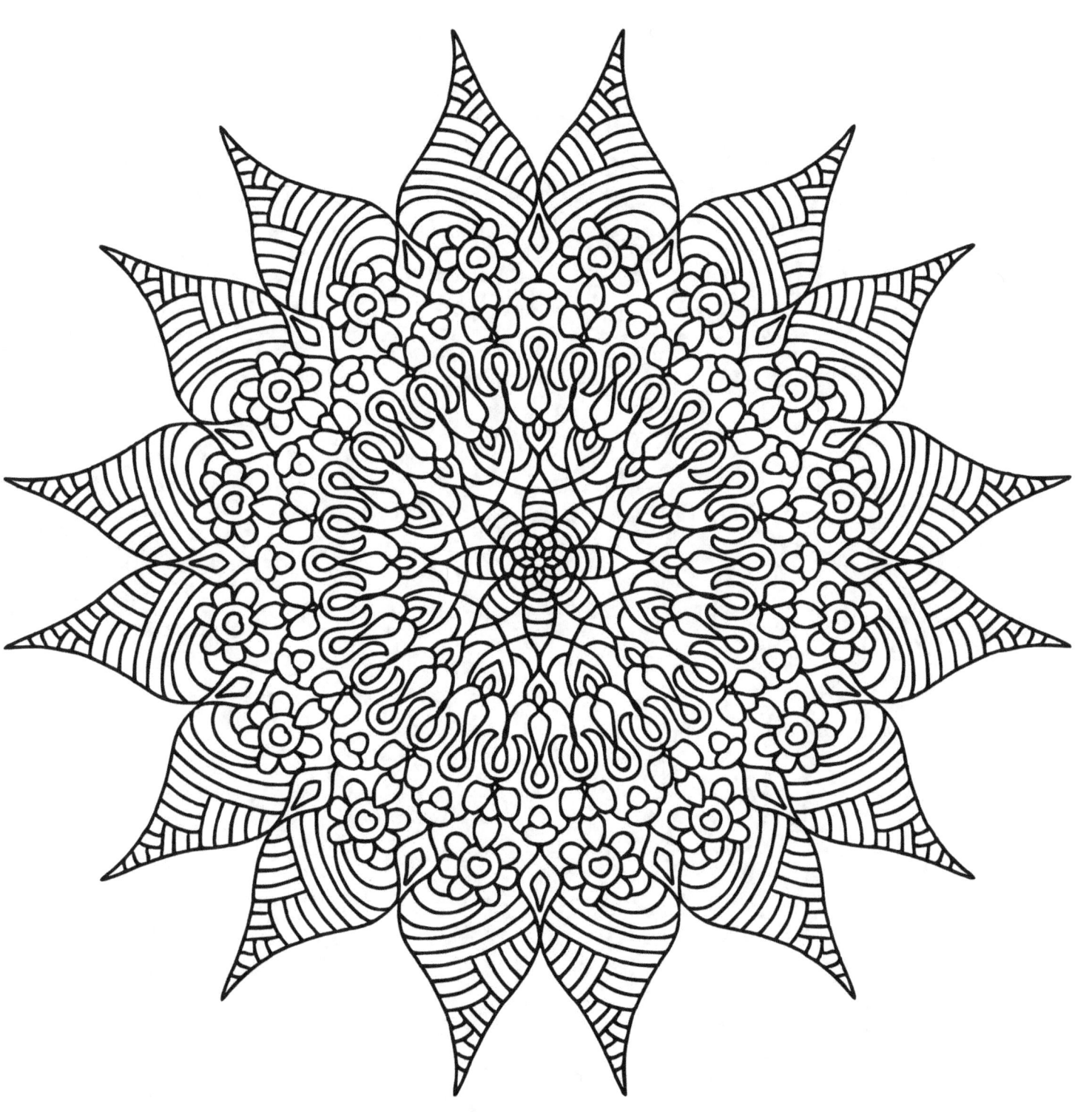

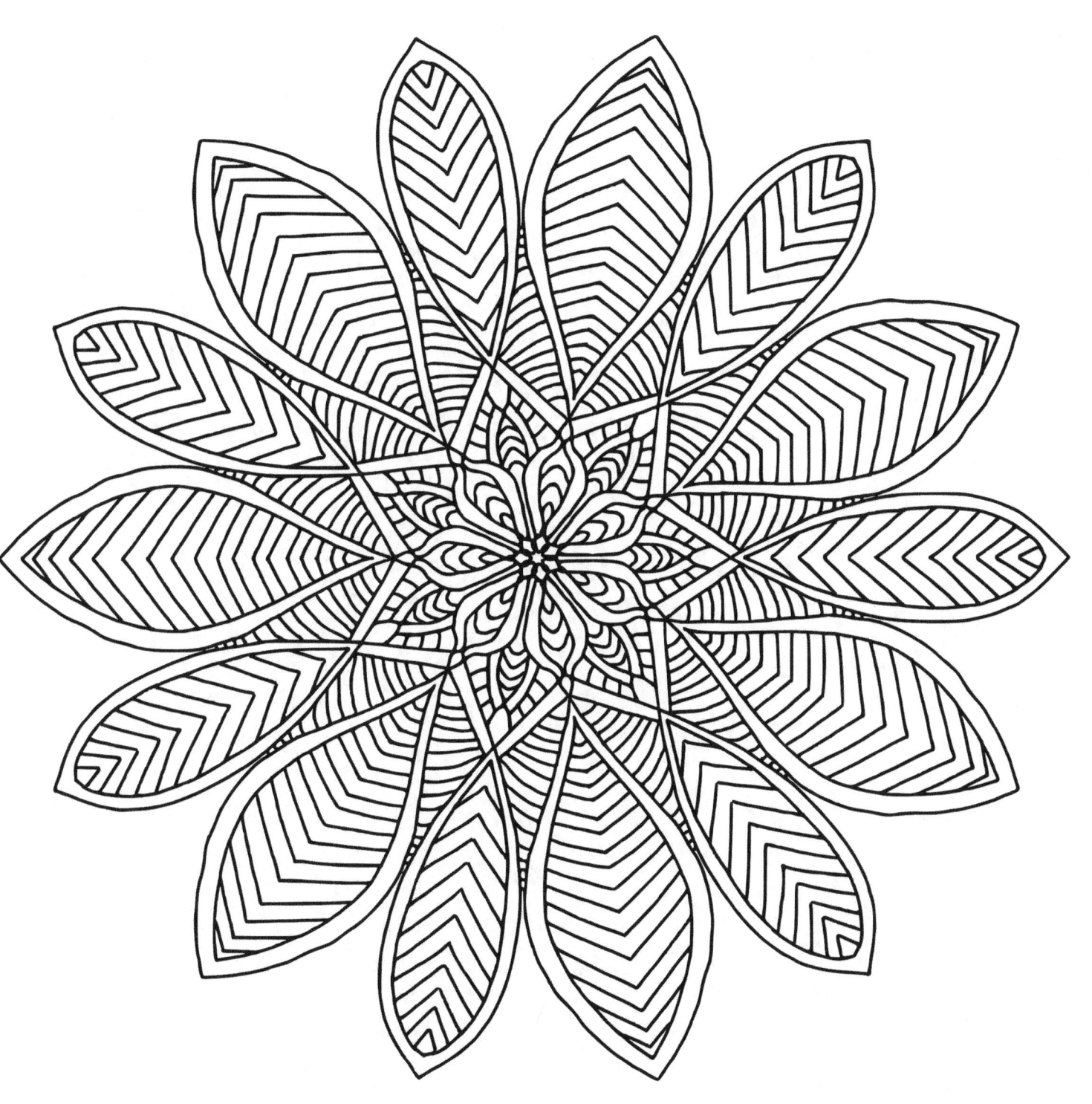

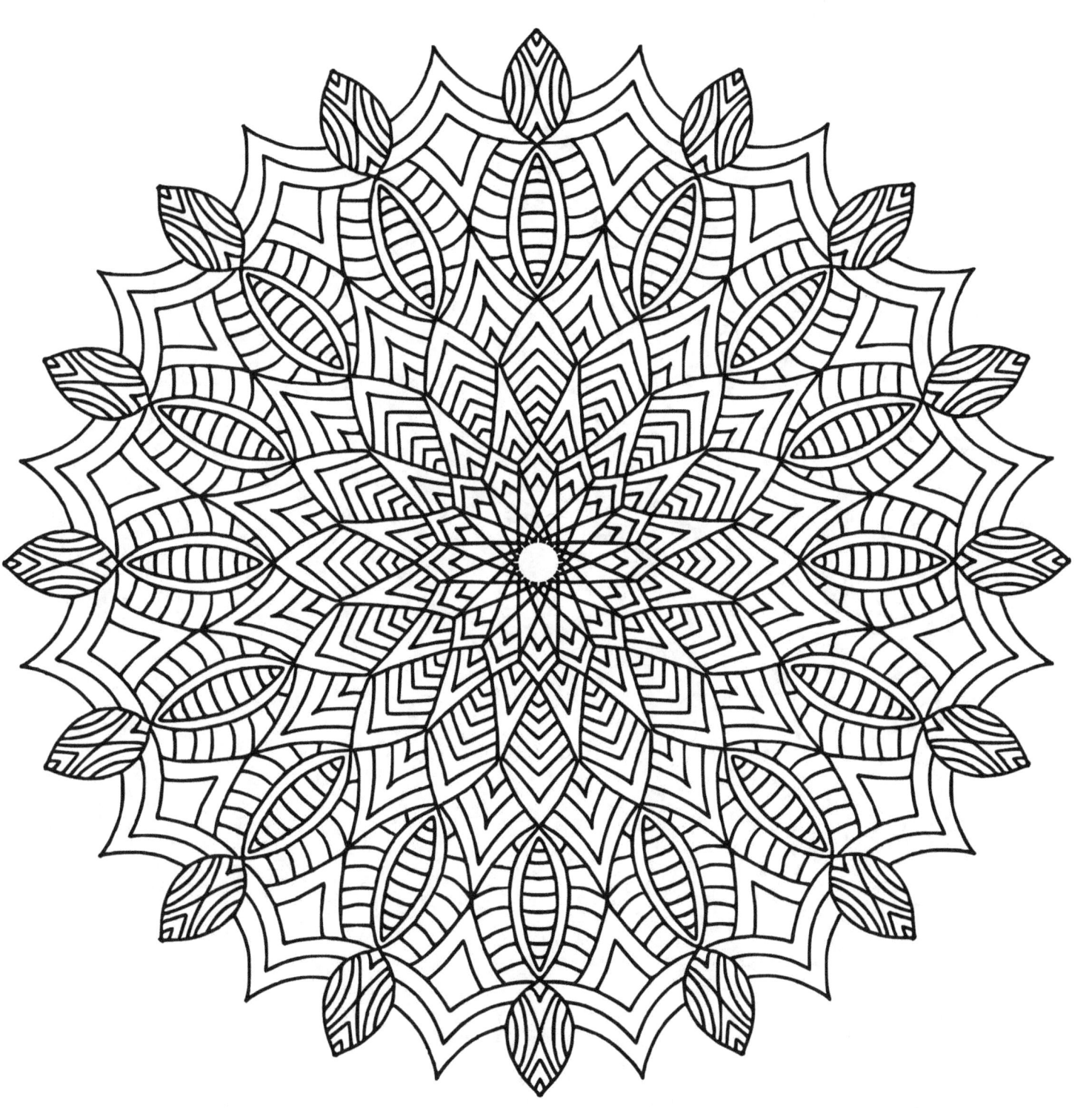

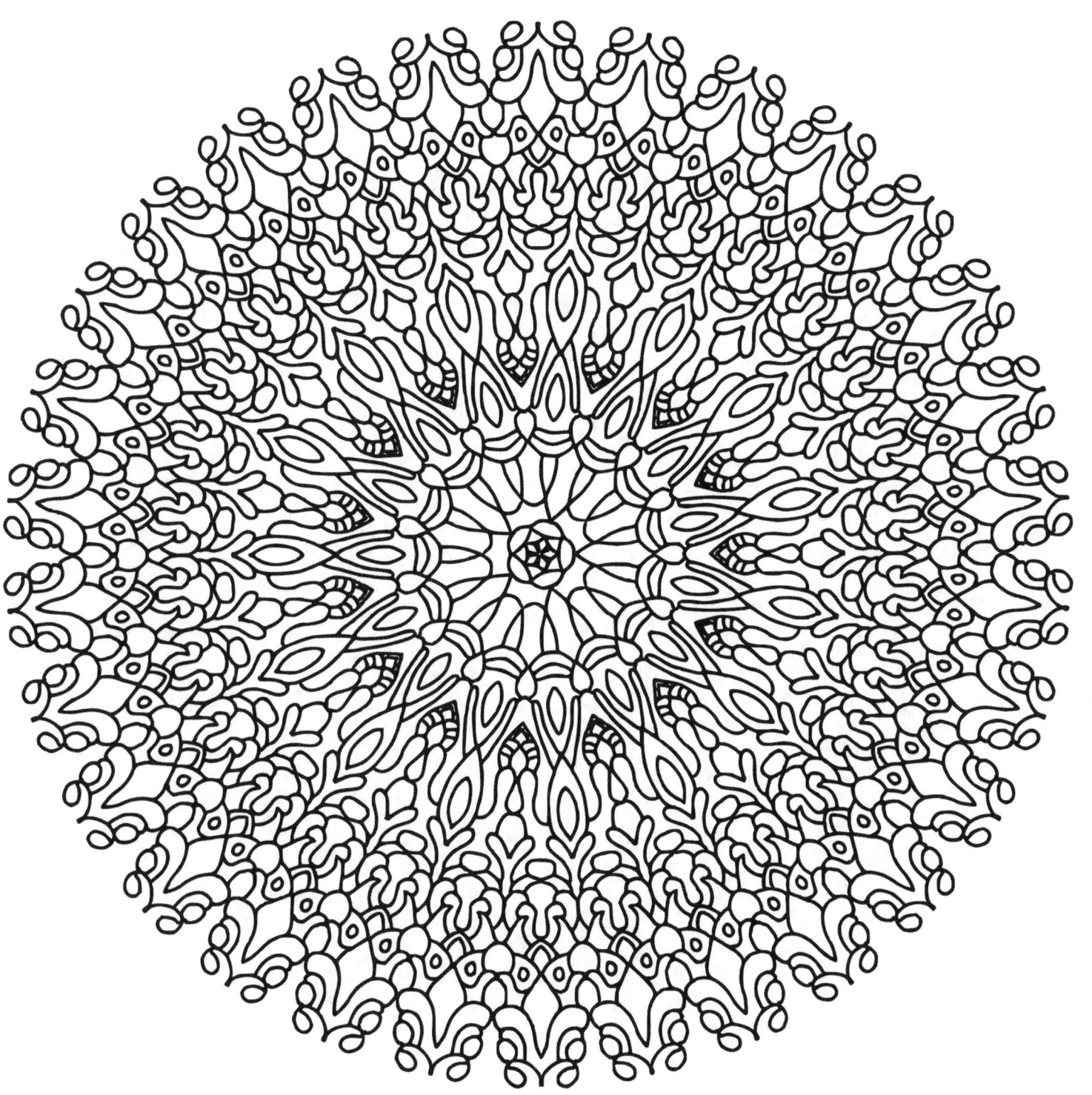

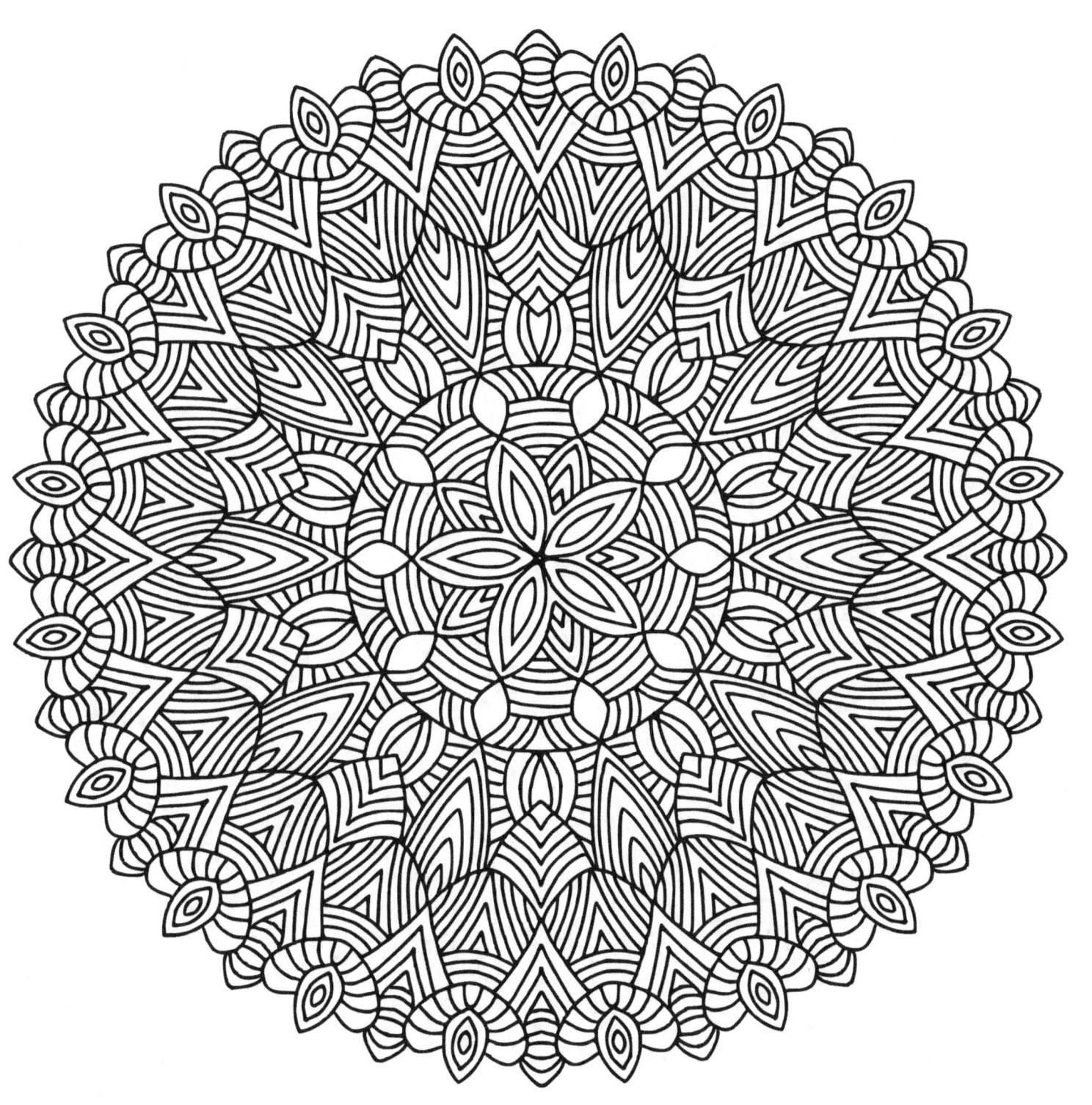

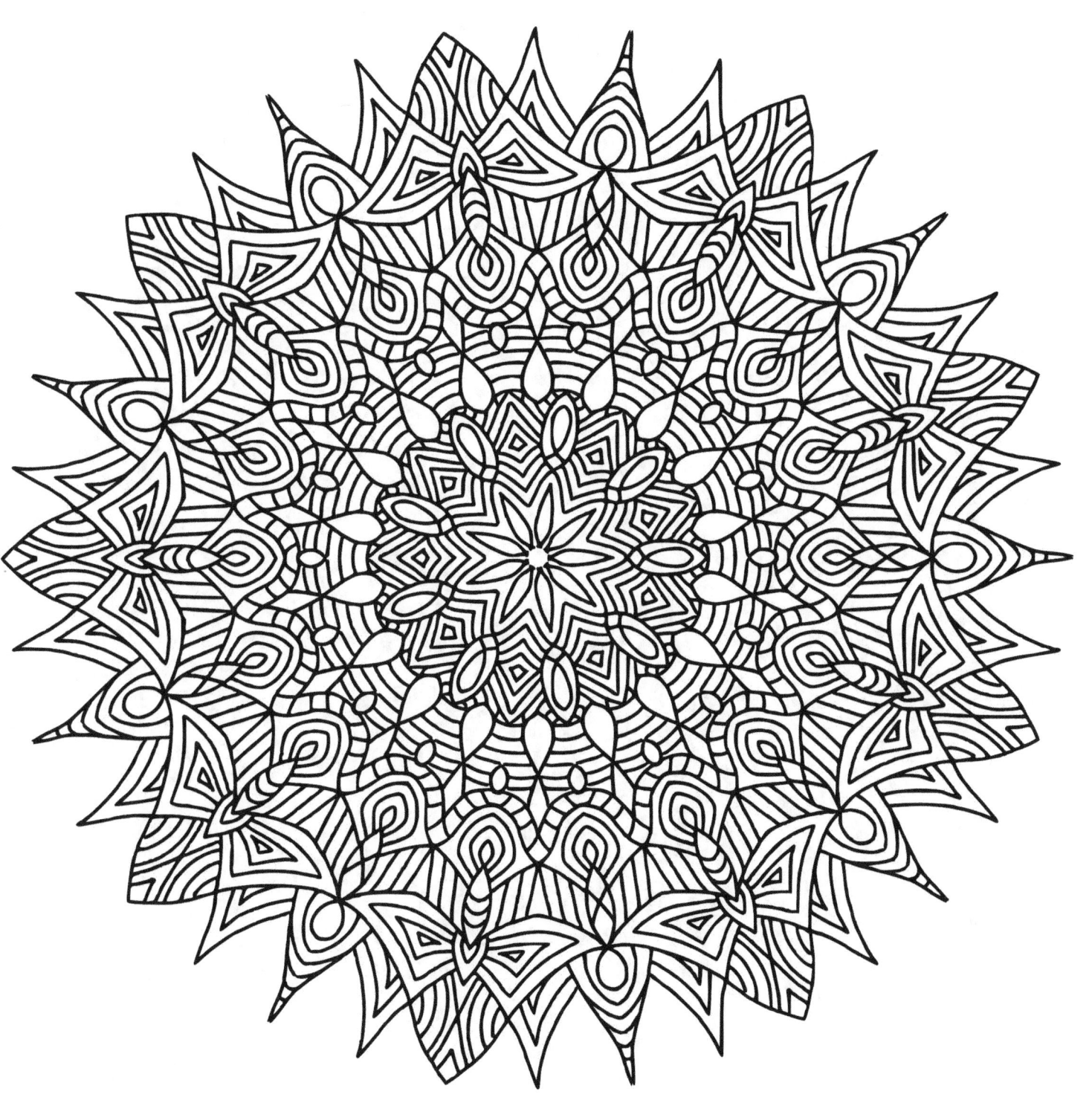

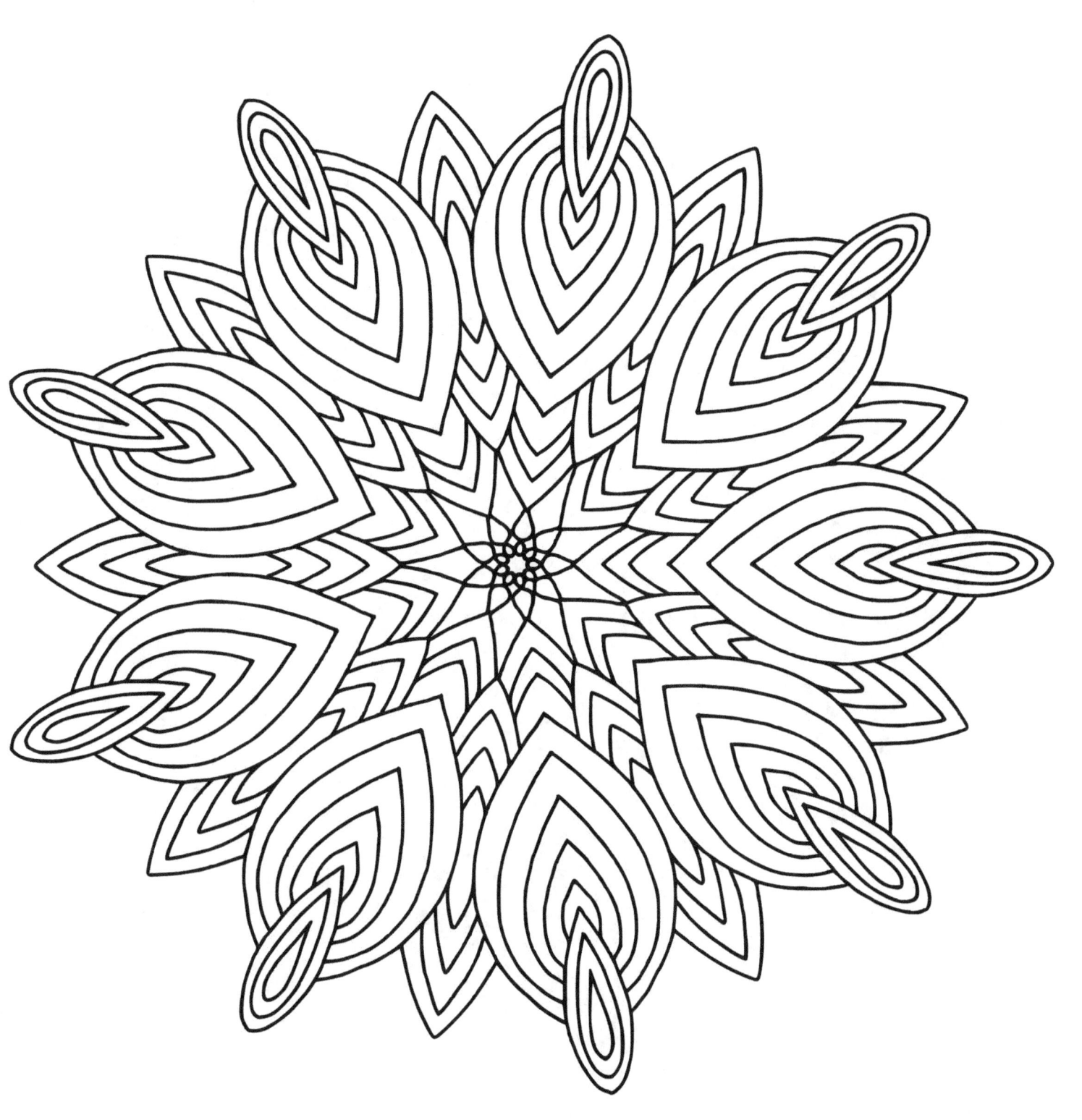

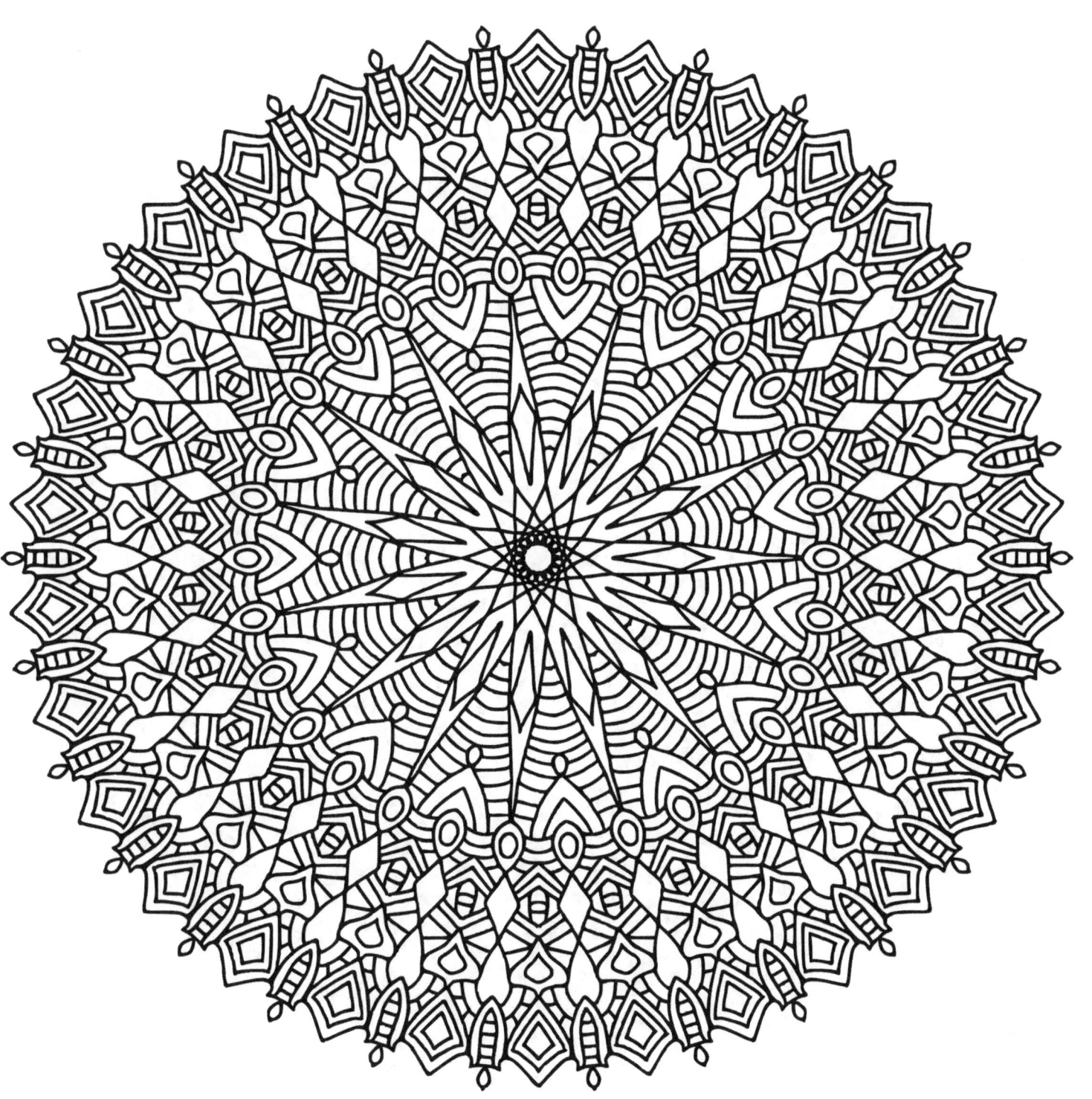

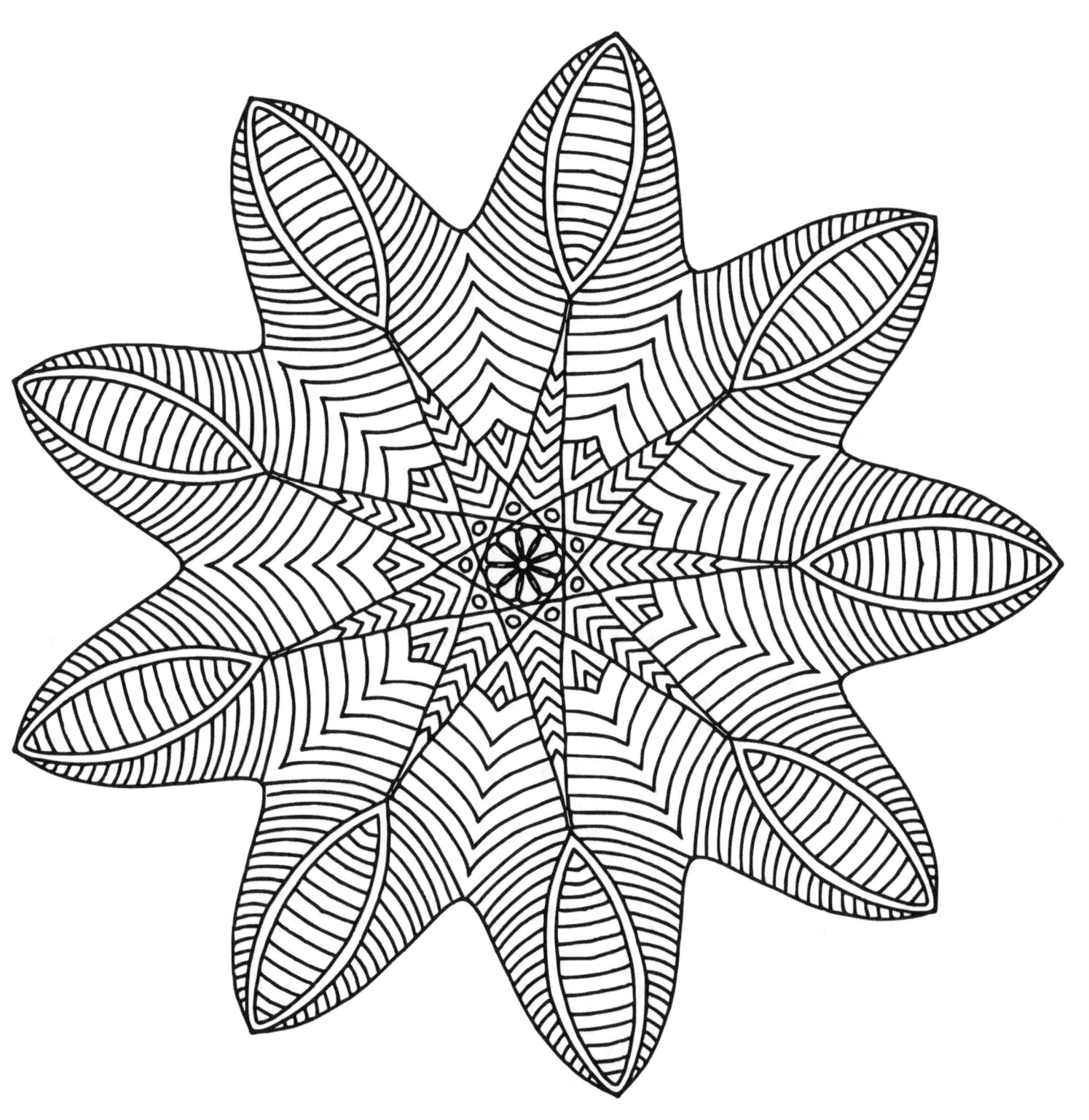

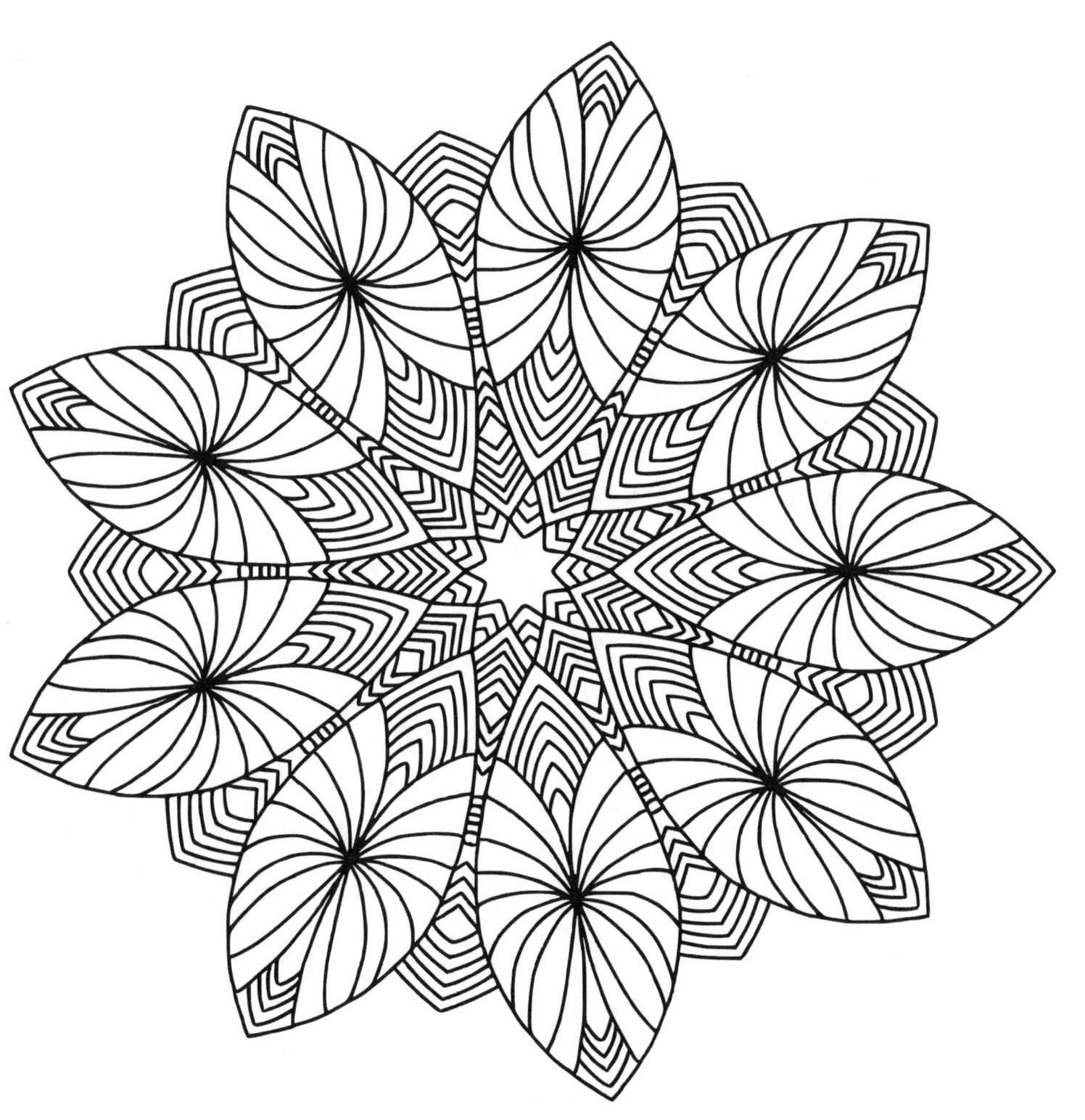

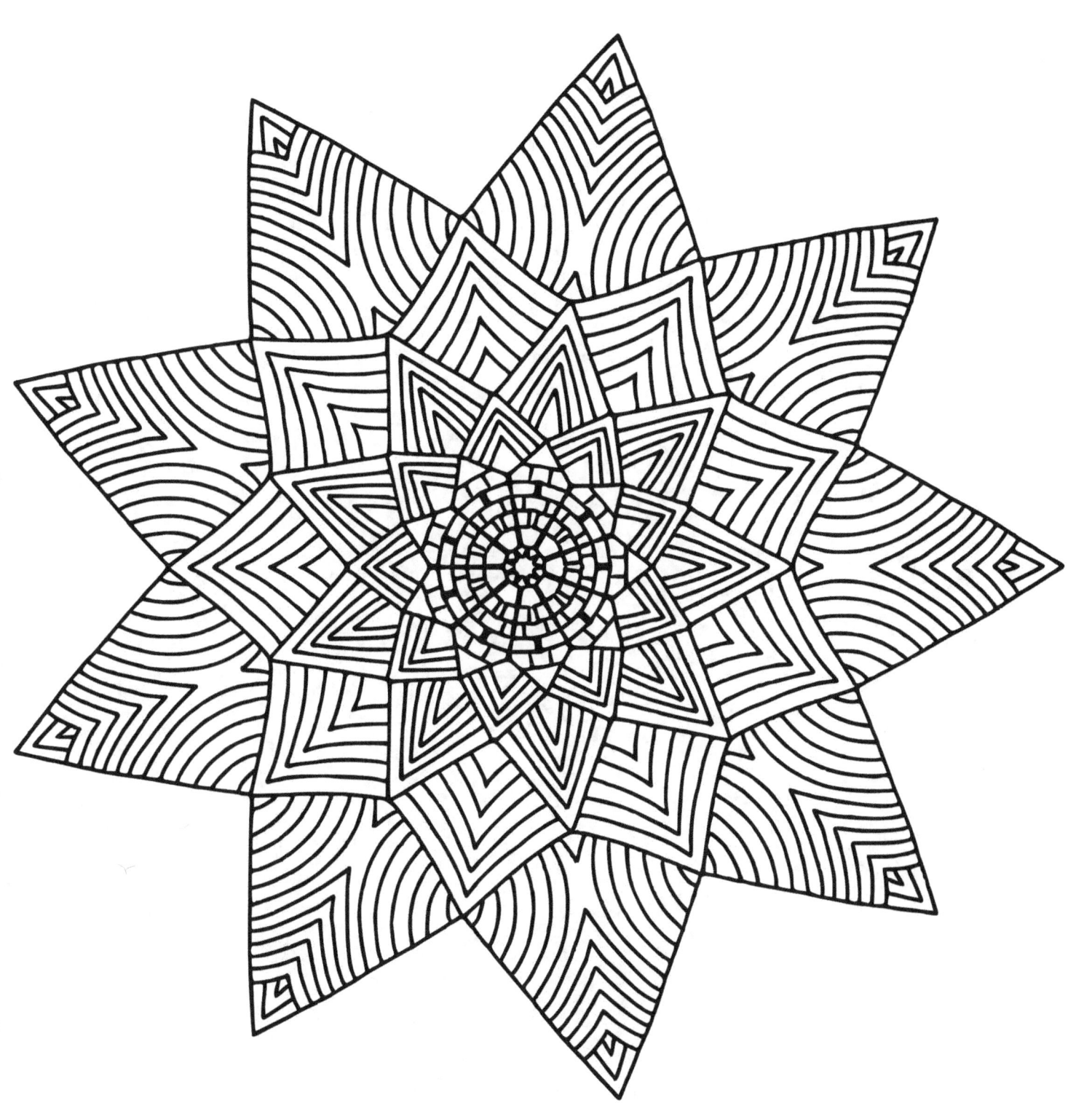

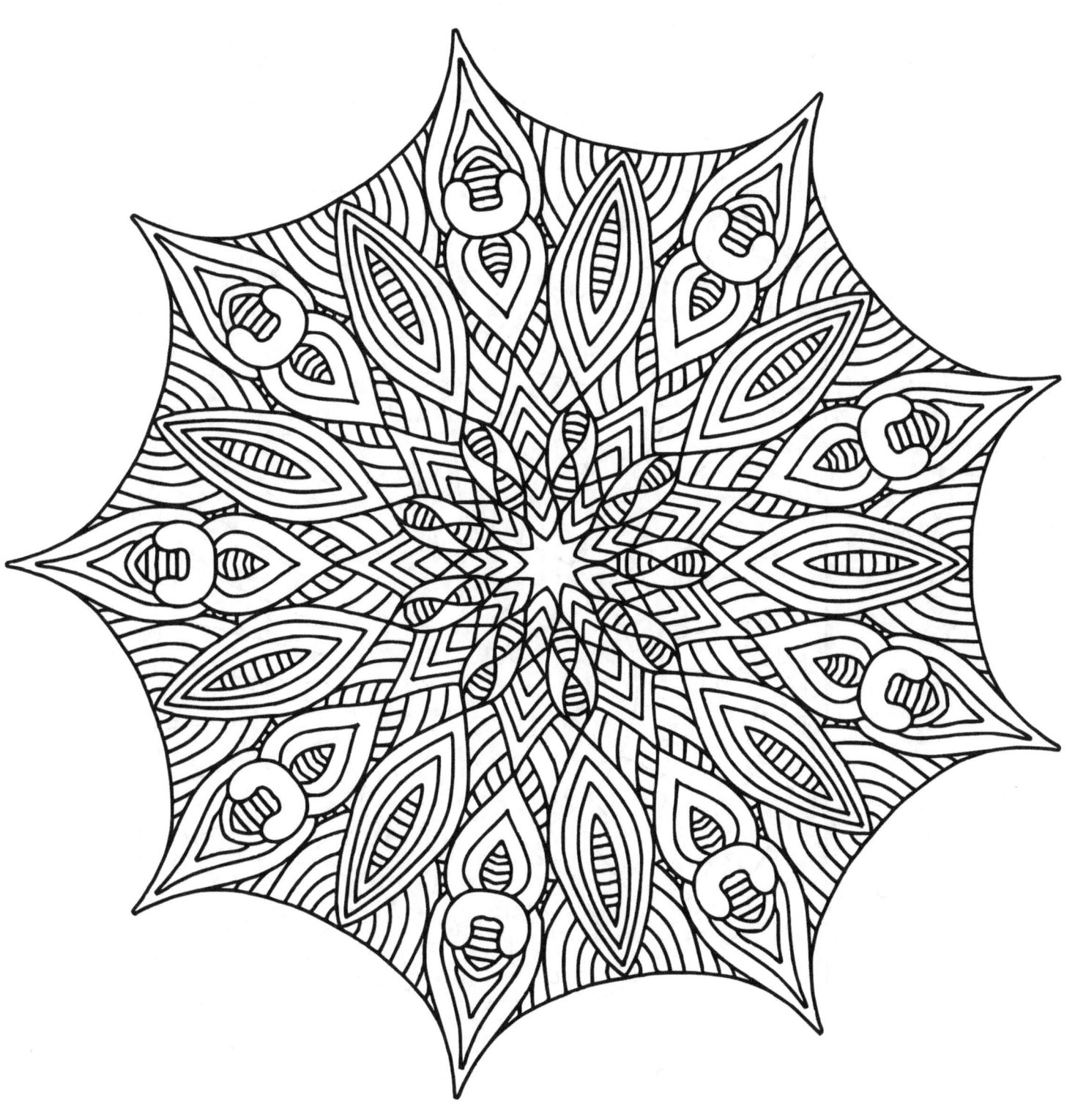

Test your colors here on the samples from
"My Pocket Coloring Companion"
&
"My Coloring Companion"

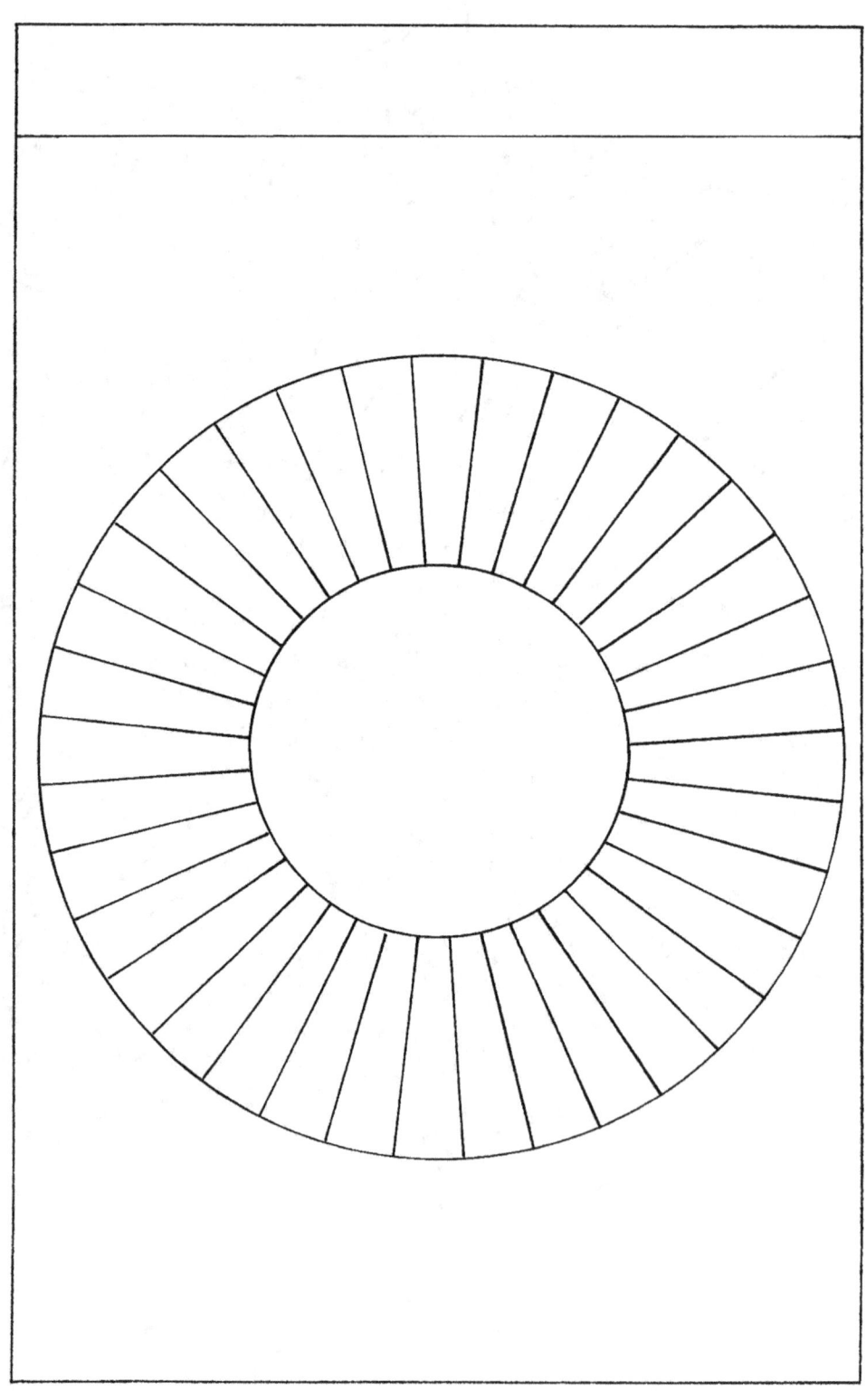

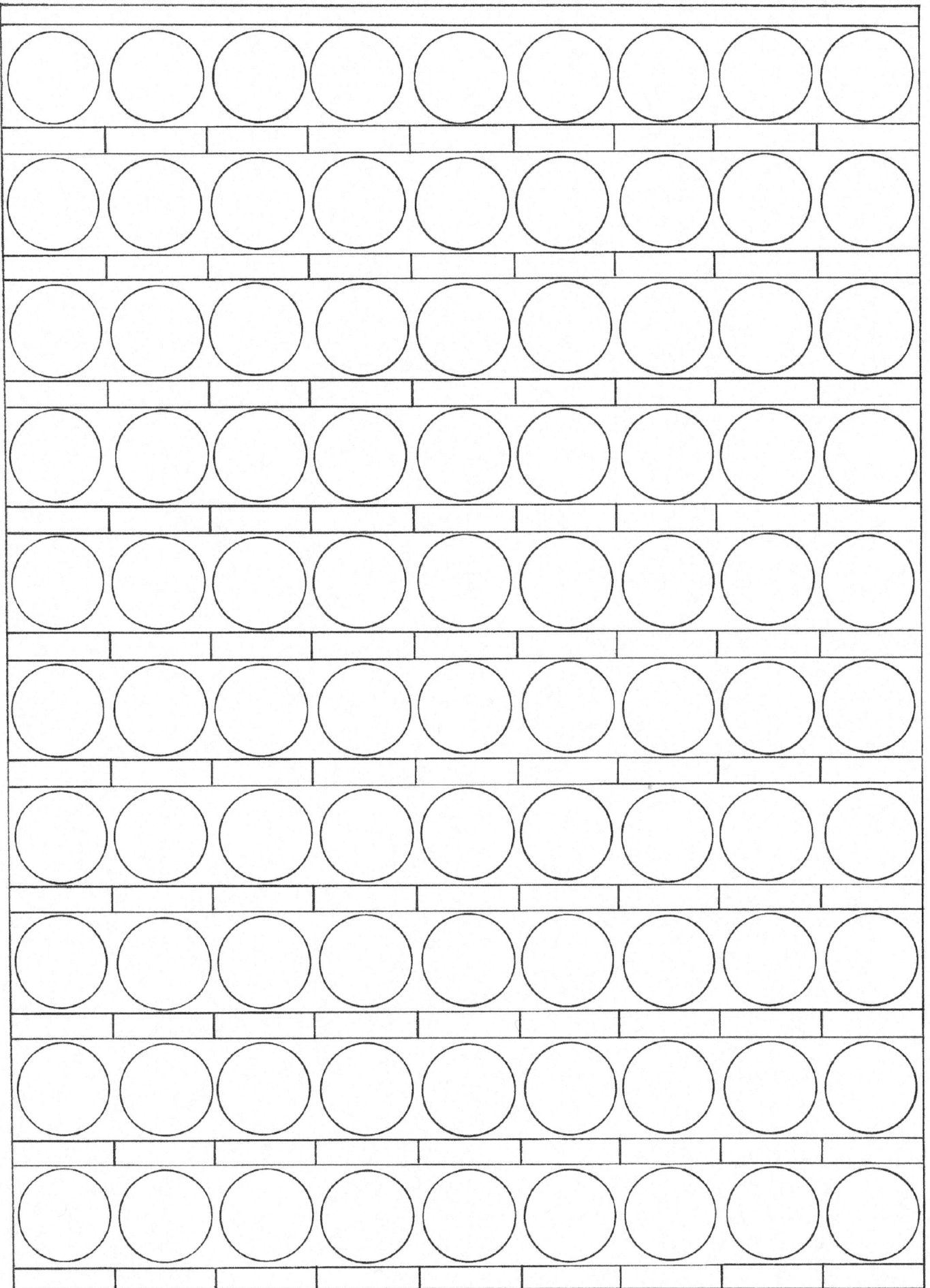

www.ingramcontent.com/pod-product-compliance
Lightning Source LLC
Chambersburg PA
CBHW081118240526
45470CB00019B/2613